WORK WITH PARENTS

The EFPP Clinical Monograph Series

Editor-in-Chief: *John Tsiantis*

Associate Editors: *Brian Martindale* (Adult Section)
Didier Houzel (Child & Adolescent Section)
Alessandro Bruni (Group Section)

OTHER MONOGRAPHS IN THE SERIES

- *Countertransference in Psychoanalytic Psychotherapy with Children and Adolescents*
- *Supervision and Its Vicissitudes*
- *Psychoanalytic Psychotherapy in Institutional Settings*
- *Psychoanalytic Psychotherapy of the Severely Disturbed Adolescent*

WORK WITH PARENTS
Psychoanalytic Psychotherapy with Children and Adolescents

edited by
John Tsiantis
SENIOR EDITOR
Siv Boalt Boethious
Birgit Hallerfors
Ann Horne
Lydia Tischler

Foreword by
Margaret Rustin

published by
KARNAC BOOKS

for

The European Federation
for Psychoanalytic Psychotherapy
in the Public Health Services

First published in 2000 by
H. Karnac (Books) Ltd., 58 Gloucester Road, London SW7 4QY
A subsidiary of Other Press LLC, New York

British Library Cataloguing in Publication Data

A C.I.P. for this book is available from the British Library

ISBN 1 85575 241 7

10 9 8 7 6 5 4 3 2 1

Edited, designed, and produced by Communication Crafts

Printed in Great Britain by Polestar AUP Aberdeen Limited

www.karnacbooks.com

ACKNOWLEDGEMENTS

I would like to express my gratitude to a number of people who have contributed significantly in the bringing of this Monograph to completion. First of all, I would like to express warm thanks to all the authors who contributed to this book. I also wish to express my special thanks to Philippa Martindale who worked hard to improve the text and reference section and to Eric King for the final copyediting. I would also like to express my thanks to the editorial committee. I am also most grateful for all the support and advice from Cesare Sacerdoti of Karnac Books. I would also like to express my thanks to Mary Kritikou and Zetta Iliopoulou for their secretarial assistance. Finally, the EFPP wishes to express its sincere thanks to the Research, Development, and Training Unit of the Special Care Department, Stockholm County Council, Sweden, for their generous financial contribution towards the costs of the production of this Monograph.

John Tsiantis
Athens, June 1999

ABOUT THE AUTHORS

ATHANASSIOS ALEXANDRIDIS (Greece) is a psychiatrist and child psychiatrist. He trained in psychiatry and psychoanalysis in France, where he worked in the public sector. He obtained his PhD from the Philosophy Department of Salonika University. He is a Psychiatrist and Psychotherapist at PERIVOLAKI Therapeutic Unit for autistic and psychotic children. Child and adult psychosis constitutes his main research and clinical interests. He has published in French and in Greek in the field of early childhood psychopathology.

BERTRAND CRAMER (Switzerland) studied medicine at the University of Geneva. He studied for ten years in the United States, where he carried out research in the field of infancy and graduated from the New York Psychoanalytic Institute. In 1970 he created the Geneva University Clinic for Child and Adolescent Psychiatry, where he became Professor. His research focuses on parent–infant communications within the framework of mother/infant psychotherapies.

MARIANNE ENGELSE FRICK (Sweden) is a social worker and trained in Rotterdam. She specialized as a child and adolescent psychotherapist at the Erica Foundation in Stockholm. She is a supervisor and lecturer within the child guidance clinics of the province of Stockholm. Until 1997 she was the Chairperson of the Swedish Association of Child and Adolescent Psychotherapists. She has published on Dutch education in psychotherapy and on require-ments of the therapeutic environment within the child guidance clinics.

VIVIANE GREEN (United Kingdom) is Head of Clinical Training at the Anna Freud Centre, London. She is a Visiting Lecturer for the Specialisation MSc course at the Department of Psychology, University of Padua, Italy. She also supervises and teaches for the University's clinical training programme. She developed a child psychoanalytic training for the Genootschap (Netherlands Psycho-analytic Institute) and supervises members. In addition, she has taught at Trinity College, Dublin, and presented papers in Prague and the Centre Alfred Binet, Paris.

ANN HORNE (United Kingdom) trained as a child and adult psycho-therapist at the British Association of Psychotherapists, London. Subsequently she became head of Child and Adolescent Psycho-therapy training at the British Association of Psychotherapists from 1994 to 1998. She is a former co-editor of the *Journal of Child Psychotherapy* and has edited, with Monica Lanyado, *The Handbook of Child and Adolescent Psychotherapy: Psychoanalytic Approaches*. She works at the Portman Clinic, London, where she is co-editor of the forthcoming Portman Series.

DIDIER HOUZEL (France) is Professor of Child and Adolescent Psy-chiatry at the University of Caen, France. He is a Full Member of the French Psychoanalytic Association. He has worked with several Kleinian psychoanalysts, in particular James Gammill in Paris and Donald Meltzer and the late Frances Tustin in London. In collaboration with Didier Anzieu, he has published papers on psychic envelopes. He has also published several psychoanalytic articles on autism and childhood psychoses.

OLGA MARATOS (Greece) studied at the University of Geneva, was assistant to Jean Piaget, and did her clinical training at Bel Air

Clinic, Geneva, and the Child Psychiatry Department at London Hospital. She is a clinical psychologist, a psychoanalyst (Hellenic Psycho-Analytical Society), and Professor at the University of Athens. She is a Child Psychotherapist and Scientific Director of PERIVOLAKI Therapeutic Unit for autistic and psychotic children. She has numerous publications in English and in Greek in the fields of newborn and early mental development, mother–infant interaction, and early psychopathology.

GILLIAN MILES (United Kingdom) is a Senior Clinical Lecturer in Social Work in the Child and Family Health Department at the Tavistock Clinic, London. She is also an adult psychotherapist.

MARGARET RUSTIN (United Kingdom) is a Consultant Child Psychotherapist at the Tavistock Clinic, London. She trained at the Tavistock and has been a member of the senior staff there since 1971. In 1986 she became Organising Director of the Tavistock Child Psychotherapy training, and in 1993 she was elected Postgraduate Dean of the Clinic. She has co-authored, with Michael Rustin, *Narratives of Love and Loss*, and co-edited *Closely Observed Infants and Psychotic States in Children* (part of the Tavistock Book Series).

JOHN TSIANTIS (Greece) is a child psychiatrist, psychiatrist, and psychoanalytic psychotherapist. He is currently Professor of Child Psychiatry and Director of the Department of Child Psychiatry, Athens University Medical School at the Aghia Sophia Children's Hospital, Athens. He is Chairman and Founding Member of the Hellenic Association of Child and Adolescent Psychoanalytic Psychotherapy. He is a Founding Member of the European Federation of Psychoanalytic Psychotherapy, for which he served as Vice-Chairman. He has worked as a consultant with WHO, EU, and other international organizations. He is particularly interested in the development of psychoanalytically based Mental Health services for children in the public sector. Current research interests include development of child mental health promotion programmes within primary health care services and evaluation of psychodynamic psychotherapies for children.

CONTENTS

FOREWORD

Margaret Rustin

The decision to publish a volume on work with parents in this EFPP Monograph series is much to be welcomed. It will go some way to remedy the relative neglect of systematic thinking about this important area of clinical practice and to mount an intellectual challenge to more systemically based family interventions. The range of authors is suggestive of one of the reasons for the absence of much published work in their area, for it draws our attention to the multidisciplinary nature of the work. Included are contributions from child and adult psychoanalytic psychotherapists, social workers, psychiatrists, and psychoanalysts. These different professional groups very often pursue their scholarly debates within professionally defined journals and distinct professional bodies. It is therefore a great pleasure to introduce a book in which a wide range of developments within psychoanalytically based work with children and families across Europe is represented.

The chapters engage the reader in theoretical issues and comparative practice and also provide accounts of a number of innovative ways of working which will be of special interest.

There are four chapters that address a broad range of work with parents. Two of these (Rustin and Green) offer accounts of current thinking in well-known centres of excellence in and training for child psychotherapy (the Tavistock Clinic and The Anna Freud Centre). There are many points of overlap, but the clinical material and discussions also exemplify the differences in psychoanalytic emphasis in the two traditions. Perhaps this might be summarized as having a good deal to do with Rustin's interest in the infantile aspects of the parents' personalities alongside the treatment of the child, in contrast with the greater emphasis in Green's chapter on the actual child. The third British contribution (Horne) discusses work with families and complex networks where "good-enough" parenting may be a critical issue. She also writes about the fashionable notion of "partnership" with parents (quite distinct from the psychoanalytically familiar category of "working alliance") and provides examples of imaginative flexible practice responsive to changing times. Frick's contribution from Sweden reviews some of the theories of parental therapy, with considerable emphasis on the parental worker's role in monitoring the child's external environment. There are subtle and important differences of view between several of the writers about the extent to which psychotherapy for the parents as a couple, or as individuals, should be part of child and family services, and related differences with respect to the training required to provide such therapy. These themes should give rise to much lively debate.

Three chapters describe specific clinical interventions. In their chapter, Maratos and Alexandridis outline work with families undertaken as part of the total care of severely disturbed children attending a therapeutic day unit. Their mixed model emphasizes securing the cooperation of parents and starts from the parents' conscious desire for help and change, moving on to tackling the negative if progress is not sustained. They attempt in particular to renew a sense of rhythm in family life. Houzel's chapter, about work with the parents of autistic children, represents a rather different approach. He argues forcefully for a model of parents as co-therapists with whom he tries to build a very particular form of therapeutic alliance. The exceptional range of specialized experience he brings to the work is evident in the great clarity of his model, which includes a profound understanding of the paradoxical depression experienced by some parents whose autistic children begin to improve. This chapter provides an example of a service whose parameters are wholly consistent with the therapeutic model enunciated, and this marriage of theory and practice makes compelling reading. Cramer's chapter on mother/infant psychotherapy documents his particular style of intervention. He offers a clear and detailed account both of what he aims to do and of his techniques. He argues for the special appropriateness of brief focused intervention in the post-partum period. This is in line with the view of other writers about parent/infant work. His description of the "double agenda" of the therapist—the attention to both mother and child—makes clear how he gathers evidence for the chosen focus. A significant question not dealt with is the place of fathers in the early mother–child relationship.

Miles' chapter reports on work in a clinical research project providing time-limited psychoanalytic psychotherapy for sexually abused girls and parallel work with their parents/carers. It is an impressive, comprehensive account, emphasizing the level of difficulty among the parents and the need for patient individual (or couple) work to support the parents through their exploration of the intergenerational issues thrown up by the disclosure of their daughter's abuse. The brief clinical vignettes provide a breadth of examples which bring to life the degree of pain and stress for the families and the need for well-supported and structured work with parents. Attention is also paid to the level of support required for the professionals involved.

Three things stand out for me in the volume as a whole. First, the rich range and depth of clinical experience available to be pondered by readers makes this book a treasured source for clinicians, and also an excellent resource for training. Second, the service development implications: resources for adequate work with parents are often inadequate, despite all the apparent political will to invest in children's mental health. Last, taken as a whole, the book is a hopeful record of work in progress at the end of the century in many centres. The writers share a powerful commitment to the relevance and value of psychoanalytically based work with parents, and they provide heartening evidence of the resilience and intellectual vitality of diverse strands within this tradition.

INTRODUCTION

John Tsiantis

The idea of compiling this book was the outcome of collaboration and discussion among the colleagues and associates of the Hellenic Society for Child and Adolescent Psychoanalytic Psychotherapy and with members of the EFPP. Through that collaboration and discussion, we ascertained the need for an examination at close quarters of work with parents in child and family settings, especially in the public sector and with particular reference to children in individual psychoanalytic psychotherapy. There can be no doubt that work with parents is significant, all the way from the diagnostic phase of assessment of the child to the stage in which the child begins to enter the process of psychoanalytic psychotherapy. The pioneers of work with parents were, of course, Winnicott, Fraiberg, and Furman, and the views of Benedek, who examines parenthood as a developmental phase in the individual life-cycle, are also familiar. There would appear to be a gap in the literature where the systematization of work with parents is concerned; in addition, changes have come about, at least over the last two decades, in the way we work with parents in child and family settings. In Britain and in other countries, it was traditionally a social worker, or at best a psychiatric social worker, who saw the parents, while the child therapist worked with the child.

Little by little, however, various changes came about, including the evolution of theories about child development, modifications to the system for the training of social workers, alterations in the service structure of the state health systems in the various European Countries, the development of psychoanalytically based work with children and families on the part of mental health professionals other than social workers, and the development of family therapy as a therapeutic method. These changes altered the traditional model for work with parents which we referred to above. Furthermore, it would appear that today families are being harder hit by disintegration, difficult socioeconomic circumstances, migration, alienation, and persecution. These factors often cause a series of traumatic experiences in the early lives of children which are re-enacted within the professional systems and organizations involved in the care of children. In such cases, parental workers themselves must be good-enough parents to hold an integrating function and must be capable of putting into words the unconscious mechanisms operating in the network, thus protecting the child's therapy while at the same time striving to keep the child and the child's needs foremost in the thoughts of carers. Nor can there be any question that nowadays children with needs are often the victims of the lack of psychosocial services, of bureaucratic procedures, and of competition or failures of communication between child and adult mental health services or the judicial system—despite all the promises and efforts made to respond to the needs of children and their families. This state of affairs raises questions not only about service development, but also about the particular demands that are created in training programmes for child and adolescent psychotherapists and, more generally, for mental health professionals working with children and adolescents and their families. This book, we hope, will have the effect of expanding the literature while at the same time serving as a point of reference for colleagues working with children, adolescents, and their parents in the public sector.

Above all, this book is clinically based, affording scope for the presentation of a range of approaches employed in centres across

Europe. In the first chapter, Margaret Rustin distinguishes four main categories of work undertaken by parents whose children have been in short- or long-term therapy.

1. Supportive work with parents with the prime aim of protecting and sustaining the child's therapy.

2. Work with parents in order to support them in their parental functioning—in other words, with parents who are in need of help to make sense of their child's behaviour and relationships, and/or parents who are struggling to cope with a great deal of stress due to a variety of different circumstances.

3. Work with parents where the focus is on the change in family functioning, possibly including marital therapy or individual work on intra-family relationships or family therapy.

4. Individual psychotherapy for one or both parents, even if the original referral stemmed from a particular concern for the child.

These different types of approach to work with parents constitute a continuum, and selection of the proposed approach is a matter for the sensitivity and clinical assessment of the professionals working in the child or family setting. This categorization, though schematic, gives some idea of the type of work being done. The approach is based on the needs of the child, but also on the availability of the parents for cooperation. It is also seen as important that an assessment be made of the fragility of the parents and of their ability to work on the level proposed. In her work, Rustin emphasizes the importance of being attuned to the infantile part of the patients, through which the worker can gain access to the disturbance in adult and parental functioning which needs to be addressed. Such an understanding requires the appropriate training on the part of the parental worker, and that in turn calls for personal experience of therapy. These points are presented and discussed through clinical case material. The approach described by Rustin is typical of the practices applied at the Tavistock Clinic in London, and there can be no doubt that if workers are to be capable of carrying out the multilayered work described they must have received a satisfactory training—including, of course, knowledge of the unconscious aspects of their own psychic life and of the phenomena of transference and countertransference. Needless to say, it would be interesting to possess a record of the trends prevailing in Europe today in work with parents. One of the objectives of such a survey would be to improve the training received by colleagues working with parents in child and family settings, at least as far as the public sector is concerned.

In the second chapter, Viviane Green presents the objectives of work with parents. According to Green, the broader aim of work with parents—apart from having the parental worker cooperate with them through the vicissitudes and adversities of the child's therapy—is to facilitate the parents in investing in the effort and in the development of the psychotherapeutic process, thus enabling them to understand the child and respond to his special needs.* As Green notes, however, this presupposes an acknowledgement that parenthood is a developmental phase of the kind formulated by Furman (1966), in accordance with which the worker needs to assess to what extent the parents have been able to maintain and progress in their development relative to the child's growth. In other words, the objective of work with parents is to facilitate their understanding of issues connected with parenthood, enlisting on each occasion different capacities through the child's development in line with the child's phase-specific needs. Among these capacities, we should include the affective capacity of the parents to acknowledge that the child is not only a creature dependent on and attached to them, but also a separate and developing individual. Green introduces the theoretical dimension of work with parents through clinical examples by stressing the need for the worker to understand how the parent holds her or his child in mind, and what sort of child is harboured in the parent's mind. Such an understanding will be indicative of the degree to which the parents possess the capacities characteristic of the parenthood developmental phase, in which parents are consistently and protractedly mindful of their child, since there are cases in which the parents' own defences or internal preoccupations affect that capacity. The

---

*For simplicity, in general discussions we have used feminine pronouns for therapists and masculine pronouns for patients.

aim of the parental therapist is to help the parents to re-create the child in their minds through the therapeutic space with which the therapist provides them. If this is to be achieved, it is very important that the parental therapist or worker should conceive the child and parents in her mind in a way that acknowledges the primacy of the child–parent relationship in its complex mutuality. Inevitably, questions related to the worker's understanding of transference and countertransference phenomena come to the fore, and these in turn raise questions about the technique applied and about the training and personality of the parental therapist. Obviously, in some cases it is sufficient that these phenomena be understood, and that understanding will define the therapeutic attitude and practice of the worker without necessarily being accompanied by interpretative work on the transference and countertransference phenomena. It is interesting that Green's chapter, though its approach is different, touches on questions similar to those raised in Rustin's contribution, thus demonstrating the complexity of work with parents and the therapeutic sensitivity that parental treatment requires. *Inter alia*, it is necessary at some points to focus on parental work in the present, in relation to the child, while at others further exploration of the past, as done in adult psychotherapy, is called for. Green also discusses questions connected with the development of transference when the therapist has both the child and the parents in parallel therapy.

Ann Horne, in the third chapter, argues that the main objective of work with parents is to help them to keep their child in mind. Her approach is multifaceted and flexible, and her descriptions are rich in clinical material. Horne presents the various aspects of parental work in a variety of situations, starting out not only from the needs of the child but also from the desire and expectation of the parents to help the child. Emphasis is placed, in parallel, on the parental difficulties that may stem from their own past, from their current relationship, and from the difficulties of the child, together with those originating in the environment and in the broader network involved in caring for the child. Horne examines the impact that these factors may have on the therapeutic intervention of the child therapist with the child and/or the parents, noting that an understanding of such phenomena can facilitate interpretative intervention on the level of the child's individual psychoanalytic

psychotherapy and on that of the therapeutic intervention with the
parents or the child's network.

The various approaches specified by Horne are illustrated with
clinical examples of the following kinds:

1. When the psychoanalytic psychotherapist sees the parents so as
    to carry out the preparatory work necessary for the engagement
    of the child in psychotherapy.

2. When one aspect of the work with parents is that described by
    Dorothy Pines, in which the parents are facilitated in holding
    the child in mind and are helped to separate their own child-
    hood experiences from the needs and activities of the child. This
    is necessary work, and failure to carry it out in advance may
    explain why the proposal that the child should engage in psy-
    chotherapy is not accepted, why the child should not engage in
    psychotherapy, or why therapy can be broken off in the early
    stages.

3. When the psychotherapist sees the parents in parallel with the
    child's psychotherapy.

This last type of work, also elaborated by Green and Rustin, is
often applied with the under-5s. The impression prevailing is that
such a technique is indicated when the parents are mature enough
or are integrated, grounded parents. This technique should be dis-
tinguished from the review meetings seemed essential for the
therapist to hold with the parents during the course of therapy—
bearing in mind, of course, the stages and processes in the therapy
of the child where the timing of such meetings is concerned. The
author also points out the need to develop work with parents as
"a partnership"—a creative partnership, I would add. In fact, it
would seem that in order to achieve this partnership the therapist
needs to contain parallel feelings of envy with a twofold direction:
envy towards the creativity of the therapist and the perfect therapist-mother and child, and the parent's envy of the child's
therapist. It also seems self-evident that the purpose of the partnership is to accentuate and support the positive aspects of the
parental function and ego skills, not only where the child is concerned (in the sense of "good-enough parenting") but also towards

all the others involved in care of the child (the school, the social welfare services, etc.). In other words, there is a clear need for parental workers as well as psychoanalytic psychotherapists—especially in the public sector—to work and collaborate in a competent way with the wider network of colleagues involved in the care of the child, including colleagues from the adult world such as social workers, teachers, psychologists, and foster-parents. This type of work should, it seems, be investigated further in order to propose principles that could be applied in child and family settings across Europe.

In chapter four, Marianne Engelse Frick presents her work on some of the theories of parental therapy. She begins by dealing with the prerequisites of child therapy and parental therapy, placing special emphasis on the issue of the motivation of the parents in participating in the process of child psychotherapy, including their own engagement in therapy. This would seem to imply that the parental worker helps the parents to understand their conscious and unconscious motivation, together with the unconscious hindrances and obstacles to realization of the therapy. Engelse Frick is particularly concerned to help the parents re-create a facilitating environment in which the development of the child can unfold. No doubt the particular emphasis that Engelse Frick places on the parental therapist in monitoring the child's external environment is important. However, it is also seen as important that the therapist should help the parents to work through, in parallel, their own unconscious conflicts and problems, even if the object of this is to prevent the intervention of the parents in the commencement and continuation of the child's therapy, for as long as it is necessary. Interestingly, Engelse Frick reports that the practice in the Swedish public sector is for psychotherapy to take place either once or twice a week, as is also the practice in other European countries, although it has to be noted that there are significant differences between the two frequencies. Frequency, indeed, raises certain questions if the same model is applied in the personal-training therapeutic work with children and adolescents of the psychoanalytic psychotherapists. Clearly, if the model is also applied to the training of psychoanalytic psychotherapists, then their capacity to carry out work in greater depth with children and adolescents and their parents may be limited. This, perhaps, is the reason why emphasis is placed on monitoring the external environment, by way of contrast to the British (and other) traditions in which equal importance seems to be attached to monitoring the internal environment. The author presents some of the theories of parental therapy, paying particular attention to those of Benedek, who sees parenthood as a developmental stage in the individual life-cycle, together with other theoretical positions that supplement one another or restate earlier theories. Engelse Frick underscores the significance of the emotions of shame and guilt that parents experience in treatment, explaining the differences between them and the great importance of understanding them. In accordance with the familiar psychoanalytic theories, and with Winnicott in particular, guilt is responsible for mobilizing reparative forces in the individual, facilitating the creation of the therapeutic alliance between the parents and the therapist; when, on the other hand, there are feelings of shame, the parents feel trapped, appear to resist, and the therapeutic alliance with the therapist is more difficult to establish. One of the first issues that the therapist has to handle is how the parents feel about the referral of their child. It is truly essential, as well as being a very delicate issue, that the therapist should handle these feelings, whose understanding is undoubtedly important in commencing and continuing the child's psychotherapy. The chapter also contains a number of vignettes of therapeutic work with parents; these provide examples of management which parental workers and students of child psychotherapy will find useful.

In the fifth chapter, Olga Maratos and Athanassios Alexandridis refer to work with the parents of children who display early severe psychopathology. The work is based on the experience of two psychoanalytically trained therapists and their reflections about the problems of mental and emotional functioning faced by autistic and psychotic children. They maintain that the important aim in working with such children is to understand the meaning of their symptoms and the way they function mentally and emotionally. The authors stress the importance of parental involvement in a more global approach to the therapy of the psychotic child and of the therapeutic alliance between the parents and their own thera-

pist. A clinical vignette illustrates how the parents' deeply unconscious psychic movements and fantasies can affect their child's
involvement in the therapeutic setting. The authors conclude by
suggesting that the psychoanalytically based approach to viewing
the emotional reactions and involvement of professionals in the
therapy of psychotic children is a very helpful one.

Didier Houzel, in chapter six, argues that the gap between
the different schools of thought in understanding the pathogenic
relationships between patients and other people—as in the case
of autistic children and their parents—is caused by the presence of
fantasy relationships that are not historically accurate. As a result
of this misunderstanding, psychoanalysis has often been little
more than a reactive and trauma-based model of child psychopathology. In connection with autism, the author further suggests
that the differences have their roots in Kanner's original 1943 arti-
cle on autism and in the way it was received. Houzel questions
Kanner's conclusions and states quite succinctly the case for not
blaming the parents for the child's predicament and autistic
state.

The author also suggests that the work of the psychotherapist
with the parents of an autistic child is to invite them to speculate
about the meaning of the child's symptoms and to support them in
their search for meaning. Houzel examines the following aspects of
the therapist's work with parents: the therapeutic alliance, understanding and decoding emotional expression, assessment of the
child's progress, and working through what Houzel identifies as
the parent's paradoxical depression.

Houzel provides a clinical vignette in which he describes how
a good working alliance can be established with the parents. The
alliance, he argues, can be established during the preliminary
meetings, at least some of which should be "conjoined" meetings
with both the parents and the child. In another vignette, Houzel
describes a way of deciphering the autistic child's emotional expression. He does not agree with the hypothesis that autistic children are unable to express their feelings or display empathy with
others, which seems to be based on the concept of the theory of the
mind. He indicates that autistic children seem to be locked
in a struggle against their own feelings—which, he believes, far

from being absent or negligible, are actually extremely powerful. Houzel also suggests that we should try to work with parents, assigning them the role of co-therapists, an approach that he describes as an application of Esther Bick's method of infant observation. Under such an approach, the therapist can even visit the family home once or twice a week for hourly sessions.

Where assessment of the child's progress is concerned, Houzel stresses the importance of regular meetings to evaluate the work that lies ahead and to coordinate that being done. He suggests that it is necessary to move away from developmental norms towards signs of improved communication and mental functioning. In his work with parents, Houzel has identified a mental state for which he has coined the term "paradoxical expression", and he describes how this can be understood and used in working with the autistic child and the parents. Overall, Houzel's chapter is an excellent illustration of an innovative way to work with both the very young autistic child and the parents.

In the seventh chapter, Bertrand Cramer presents a model for psychotherapy of mother and infant focusing on conflictual parent–infant relationships which may lead to the appearance of functional disturbances in the infants.

The aim of this model of mother/infant psychotherapy is to unravel focal conflicts in the relationship to the child. It does not extend to systematic therapy involving the whole personality of the parents, as a result of which it is brief and addresses cases in which the mother does not have major pathologies. Cramer presents various clinical vignettes in which special emphasis is placed on predictions about the infants—predictions that are considered to hold valuable information about maternal representations of adult psychic functioning. These representations are also linked to the mother's own fantasies and wishes, or to representations of individuals of importance in the mother's own life. In Cramer's work, as in classic brief focal therapies, the active search is then to find a central constellation as the focus that the therapist tries to capture. The central constellation is triggered by the mother–infant interaction. Definition of the focus itself is based mainly on the process of projective identification, as well as on the special state that the mother finds herself in during the post-partum period. At that time, the mother may experience regressive

identifications and will also be propelled by positive forces to create a positive and protective relationship to the baby. The mother's
positive forces, and her strong motivation to protect and nurture
the baby (which allows her to identify, consciously and unconsciously, with the baby), are equivalent to Winnicott's primary
maternal preoccupation, which is in force during this period.
Cramer undoubtedly makes good use of this very sensitive period
in the mother's life. It would seem that a special profile of the
mother/infant therapist—and, I would add, a particular talent—is
required, demanding *inter alia* that the therapist has received full
training in adult and child therapy as well as special training in the
approach discussed in the chapter. For precisely these reasons,
however, and although the approach is very useful in furthering
our understanding of early mother–infant relations and disturbances as well as psychic structure, one wonders how easily it
could be exported for application in the public health services of
Europe and elsewhere.

Among the interesting aspects of this type of work is the fact
that, in accordance with the principle of evidence-based work, one
can study the therapeutic processes as they take place.

The closing chapter covers the work being done by parental
workers with parents whose children had been sexually abused
and had engaged in time-limited individual or group therapy.
Gillian Miles introduces her chapter by portraying the complex
feelings aroused in abused children and their mothers by the act of
sexual abuse, together with the impact of sexual abuse on the
internal world of the non-abusing parent (the mother, since the
paper deals only with the abuse of girls by male offenders).

After presenting some brief vignettes, Miles describes a wide
range of issues related to trauma, family history, parenting, the
family, and the culture. These issues include:

1. The trauma of the non-abusing parent.

2. The girl's attachment to the abusing father.

3. The mother's conflict over maintaining her marriage and her
    relationship to the abusing father, which makes it difficult for
    her to comprehend the extent of the trauma suffered by the
    child, with its concomitant anxiety and pain.

4. The fact that the mothers of the children may themselves have suffered transgenerational abuse from their parents or other persons.

5. The mother's difficulty in providing a safe basis for the child when her own life lacks a stable and reliable attachment figure.

6. The presence of challenging behaviour in the sexually abused child (sexualized behaviour, on the one hand, or intense withdrawal and feelings of lack of self-worth, on the other).

7. The understanding and management of the countertransference feelings evoked in the parental care workers as a result of the feelings projected powerfully by the families in which the abuse occurred.

8. The acknowledgement that sexual abuse evokes painful feelings in the worker and can disrupt the worker's capacity to think, thus necessitating supervision.

9. The need to work with the community network involved in the care and management of the child (social workers, members of the staff of residential settings, foster-parents, teachers, etc.).

Miles then moves on to examine the therapeutic quality of the role of the parental care worker and the worker's need to bear in mind the boundaries of the treatment and psychoanalytic psychotherapeutic work with the child, not to mention the child's continuing safety. Miles notes that the parental care worker must support the mother in her role and contain the emotions of shock, despair, and confusion stimulated by disclosure of the sexual abuse. When the mother has the strength to do so, it is necessary that with the help of the parental worker she should be able to link these emotions with her own earlier experiences of deprivation, abuse, and trauma. The time-limited help given to the parents described by Miles was undoubtedly important and facilitated the psychotherapeutic work with the children. Furthermore, it becomes apparent that these parents, the majority of whom were also severely deprived and traumatized, received at least a certain amount of help in resolving some of their difficulties, although they would unquestionably have needed prolonged additional assistance. This, of course, reveals the shortcomings of the help provided by the public health system, reflecting, more generally, the failings of the social policy and care system towards such families, whose lives bear the stamp of a wide range of social and economic adversities and the trauma and deprivation imposed by neglect and by physical, sexual, and emotional abuse.

The themes dealt with in this book are the result of many years of investigation and clinical research by colleagues from different parts of Europe. We hope that this record of their experience will help the further development of psychoanalytically based work with children and families in Europe. At the same time, it may serve as another useful tool for students of child and adolescent psychoanalytic psychotherapy.

Editor-in-Chief
January 2000

CHAPTER ONE

Dialogues with parents

Margaret Rustin

This chapter is intended as an overview of current practice at the Tavistock Clinic. The approach described also represents a significant strand within child, adolescent, and family mental health services of the British National Health Service. I shall sketch a map of some varieties of approach, provide clinical examples, raise some ethical concerns, and explore how work with parents is encompassed within the identity of the child psychotherapist.

History of work with parents within child guidance

Perhaps it would be useful to start with some historical background. The early generations of child psychotherapists could rely on close working partnerships with experienced social workers

---

A paper on which this chapter is based was presented at the Annual Conference of the Association of Child Psychotherapists in March 1997.

(Harris, 1968). The postwar child guidance clinics were fortunate in their genuine multidisciplinary ethos and particularly in their social workers, who usually had a commitment to a psychoanalytically based understanding of human development and family relationships. Much of Winnicott's writing about his hospital work is imbued with his sense of the multidisciplinary teams within which his creative potential developed and standards of good practice were established. This was a very particular culture of care.

The child cases I took on during my training and in the early years after qualification were often supported by either long-term work with the mother of the referred child or work with the couple, where the focus might be on the couple's relationship. Psychiatric social workers had the skill of bearing the actual child in mind while finding ways to address the anxieties of parents (Shuttleworth, 1982). Their work tended to be on the borderline of case work (by this I mean work intended to support parental functioning) and psychotherapy. Proper use was made of the transference as a source of evidence of emotional conflicts, but it was rather rarely used explicitly. However, during this period there was a sea-change going on in the training and professional framework of social work, which was eroding such forms of practice. By the late 1970s, interest in internal aspects of relationship difficulties had waned and family therapy was the dominant therapeutic tool of interest to social workers. Child psychotherapists had to rethink how to approach work with parents.

The approach of child psychotherapists

This situation led to many of us seeing the way forward as one in which we would need to be able to support each other's cases. It was frequently noted that unless long-term work with parents was provided, the child's therapy was at risk of interruption, irregular attendance, and so on. Who better to provide the necessary input than one of our own colleagues? However, this development raised important questions of technique. We were very carefully trained in working within the psychoanalytic model of observation of transference and countertransference phenomena, and the interpretation of unconscious material, with insight as a primary goal of the work, but this kind of approach was by no means always appropriate or acceptable to parents. So we had to learn to use our observations of underlying patterns of object relations in different ways. We also found ourselves exposed to shaky marriages, borderline personalities, the risk of adult psychotic breakdown, perverse family structures, and so on; all of these, while they could be approached coherently on the basis of the training in work with children and adolescents, also took us into new territory. I do not think we have fully resolved the consequences of this either in terms of training or in thinking deeply enough about the clinical issues. Seminars in work with parents are a requirement in the Tavistock training, but often this work can be very difficult indeed. Does the absence of an expectation of individual supervision reduce the attention given to this work and its status? Is the work done of an adequate quality? Perhaps our anxieties on this score are one source of the tendency for child psychotherapists to go on to train as adult therapists or analysts. There are often excellent reasons for people seeking this extension of their professional capacities, but possibly some of the pressure to seek further training is a consequence of our not having solved the problem of how to train for the component of adult work within any child psychotherapist's practice.

A possible model

In reviewing the range of work undertaken with parents, I have come to think about four main categories. At one end of the spectrum are cases where gaining the support of parents to protect and sustain the child's therapy is the prime aim. The second group is where parents are looking for support in their parental functioning. The development of brief work with the parents of babies and small children is a specialization within this category (Daws, 1989; Miller, 1992). This group includes parents who feel they cannot make sense of a child's behaviour and relationships and who seek a better understanding of their children's problems, and parents who are struggling to cope with very difficult life circumstances—

family illness, economic stress, disability, bereavement, and so on. These parents either see themselves as working in partnership with the professionals or feel in need of help themselves, but with the focus clearly on their role as parents. The third group is where the explicit aim of the work is change in family functioning, and this has been agreed by the parents as part of the treatment as a whole. There are different styles of work which may be appropriate, including marital therapy, individual work with a focus on the intra-family relationships, or family therapy as such. At the other end of the spectrum is individual psychotherapy for one or indeed both parents, to which the parents have committed themselves as patients in their own right, even if the issues that have brought them into contact with psychotherapists have started off as concern for a child. Both the therapies aimed at change within the family and psychoanalytic psychotherapy can function either alongside treatment of a child or on their own. I fully realize that these categories are schematic and that clinical cases often face us with work that veers between one or another type of work, but I think that it may be useful nonetheless to have the broad range subdivided. Sometimes the move from one position to another on this spectrum needs to be not only grasped by ourselves but also rendered explicit to patients. It is a bit like the transition from assessment into ongoing therapy. If work in progress makes it clear that a different aim from that originally intended is appropriate, signalling this can both give us real consent for a change in technique and enable us to free ourselves from confusion about what we are responsible for. My examples will address some of these points further.

First clinical example

Let me take first the support of a child's treatment. A recent example comes vividly to mind. An 8-year-old boy was about to begin three-times-weekly treatment. His evangelical Christian parents are separated. Both are closely involved with their two children. The boy had previously attended a one-year children's group therapy, and his mother had joined a parallel parental group of which she spoke with warmth. She then requested individual help for herself and had been offered weekly sessions. The father, Mr A, however, needed to be catered for in addition. The parents' relationship is stormy, full of writs and injunctions as well as real efforts to share out the care of the children. Mr A has a tendency to manic-depressive episodes and has made a serious suicidal attempt. He is under the care of a psychiatrist and also has had some counselling arranged as part of his psychiatric care. He has shown himself to be very touchy indeed about being treated as of equal importance to his wife in relation to his son. Faxes to the chief executive with complaints about clinic staff are part of the fat file that I inherited at the point where a tutee of mine was to take on the boy's therapy. What should we offer this father? Seeing the potential for trouble, I decided that a very clear-cut approach would be best. I offered Mr A an initial meeting in my role as Case Consultant—this is the title given at the Tavistock to the clinical manager of a case. In this I negotiated that I would be seeing him together with his son's therapist (a young man for whom this was a first intensive case) each term, to review the progress of the psychotherapy. If anything arose in between these meetings, Mr A was invited to get in contact with me. Despite the alarming tone of the threats that Mr A uttered in his initial meeting with me (he announced that he would not hesitate to consult his lawyer or to complain to all relevant authorities if he felt in any way left out of any decisions about his son's treatment, or indeed mistreated in any other way), Mr A has in fact been supportive of the boy's therapy overall and has taken a share in bringing him to sessions.

My feeling was that a number of factors had to be taken into account: first, this father needed to feel taken seriously as having parental responsibility and not dismissed as mentally ill; second, he needed the clinic to provide an absolutely clear account of who was responsible for what, particularly since the prior management of the case had been rather confused; third, the responsibility for containing Mr A had to lie with a senior member of staff who had the confidence to stand up to potential bullying and who would be seen as having authority both by the family and by the members of the clinical team. As psychotherapists, we usually veer away from taking an authoritative stance, but I think that there are circumstances where the assertion of professional authority is appropriate, when it is based on knowledge and a willingness to take responsibility. This can be the best containment of an unstable parent.

Parents who seek support

Now let us look at work with parents where they are openly seeking support. I would like to refer to two contrasting cases, both concerning the parents of autistic children. It should be mentioned that this group of parents is one with special needs, both because of the complexity of the network of services with which their child is likely to be involved and because of the peculiar loneliness often felt within these families (Klauber, 1998). Their children are so difficult to understand and to integrate into social life. One helpful approach tried out by Sue Reid and Trudy Klauber (colleagues at the Tavistock Clinic developing new approaches to work with families with an autistic child) was the establishment of a group for these parents, meeting once a term or so for an extended evening meeting, during which some of their shared concerns could be discussed. Parents felt helped by each other in coping with family and community issues. This group was in addition to the regular work undertaken with them on a case basis.

To undertake supportive work with parents, two possible models can be considered. The first is when the child's therapist also works with the parents. This can be seen as an extension of the termly review meetings, and is appropriate when the parents seem very reluctant to see anyone else. It may, of course, also be the only option available in the context of limited resources. When the referred child is psychotic or autistic, there can be good reasons for parents wishing to maintain a close contact with the child's therapist. She is often the person most able to help them understand the very puzzling character of their child's behaviour, and if some understanding of bizarre rituals or explosive tantrums can be achieved, it is easier for parents to sort out their response (Tischler, 1979).

Second clinical example

In my work with a psychotic girl, "Holly", whom I saw for psychotherapy for nine years, starting from when she was aged 13, I found that the work with her parents—which I had taken on reluctantly—was in fact fruitful, although I had started out by wishing that they would accept my offer to find them a colleague who would see them regularly. As they gained confidence in my commitment to working with this very ill girl, saw that I could make some sense of her behaviour and communications, and would take seriously how immensely burdensome her illness was to all the other members of the family, they began to give up some of their defensiveness. The mother in particular had told a tale of extensive prior contact with professionals, by whom she felt blamed for Holly's autism; in fact, in the early years she had been told that she was the one who needed psychiatric treatment, as it was her anxiety, not anything in her child, that was the problem. Her conviction that I recognized the agonies that Holly endured, and also appreciated how painful it was to be close to her and feel responsibility for her, was the basis of increasing trust in me.

I met these parents once or sometimes twice each term throughout Holly's treatment. Occasionally, these meetings also included at the parents' request another professional with responsibility for an aspect of Holly's life. For example, a local authority social worker who became involved in relation to possible residential placement when Holly was 18 joined us; later, when Holly moved to live in the community, the nun in charge of the institution that Holly joined, a woman with immense good sense and a capacity to enjoy the good qualities of damaged young people, also came from time to time. The parents saw me as Holly's interpreter on these occasions, with the task of making sure that other professionals had a proper grasp of what sort of person she was. They also valued my willingness to speak up for facing the realities: they often felt subjected to pressures to agree to what they felt was against Holly's interests—in particular, to deny the extent of her pain and her illness and to adopt a spurious cheerfulness about her future.

In the work with the parents themselves, there were four major areas where useful work was done, and one where I felt defeated. This last was in my efforts to create space for consideration of Holly's younger sister, for whom I felt concerned, but I never succeeded in this.

The first matter we tackled was to explore what could be done about Holly's ruthless splitting of the parents. She rejected her mother systematically and indeed all things female, while idealizing her father, who was an art teacher. She spent hours entrancing him with what he saw initially as remarkable creativity. This consisted mostly in model-making, at which she was deft, the models being delusional penises (lighthouses, windmills, etc.) which she made by the dozen. These were felt by her to support her absolute denial of her own femininity. Her hatred and mistrust of her mother was painfully recognized by the mother as in part a response to the mother's hatred of her in her early years. This mother's sense of rejection, faced with an autistic baby, combined disastrously with fear rooted in the history of mental illness in her family of origin to create a pool of hatred, which she knew she had been unable to contain. But the vengefulness of Holly's refusal to recognize the loving and devoted side of her mother needed a change of stance from her father: he had to stand up to her distortions, as well as to challenge his own narcissistic pleasure in being the preferred parent. My involvement in the overall care of Holly resurrected respect for the maternal role, allowed the mother to regain some sense of her importance to Holly, and allowed the father to give back to her some of his ill-gotten gains and to share with her the heaviness of the task of confronting Holly at times. The reversal of roles had been at the expense of the mother's capacity for tenderness and of his capacity for firmness.

A second focus was on how Holly might be shifted from her defensive obsessional rituals. Over the years, as the family gained more confidence in me, they were able to turn to me for help in gathering courage to assert themselves against her deadening demand for sameness. They ultimately rebelled against the tyranny of having to go on the same bus ride, have the same meals on predictable days of the week, and answer the same questions for the thousandth time. Their conversations with each other and me enabled them to see that Holly's belief that she would fall to pieces if her will was challenged was unreal. Her tantrums had been so explosive and so overwhelming to them that they had boxed themselves into a shared phantasy about Holly's need to be treated as tenderly as an egg, as though her identity were a shell always at risk of shattering. Related to this process of becoming empowered as parents and escaping from Holly's rigid control was their struggle to assert themselves against the maternal grandmother, who had maintained a malignant idealization of Holly which overlooked her capacity to devastate others' lives as well as her own. Holly's mother found in me an ally to sustain her against the denigratory and envy-loaded projections of her own mother and against her daughter's projections of despair, meaninglessness, and unending guilt. Discussing the details of Holly's peculiar preoccupations sometimes enabled them to find meaning in what had become unthinkable about, because it was so strangely impenetrable. They became more able to distinguish between what had valuable meaning and was worth listening to and pondering and what was fundamentally an attack on meaningfulness and required parental limit-setting. Family life had been shaped by an anxiously compliant respect for Holly's problems, which needed to come into question. For example, when she asked for the hundredth time for reassurance that she would not have to share a room or a bed with her sister on the family holiday, was it constructive to answer as if this were a reasonable question, or was it reasonable to express irritation and refuse to go along with her claim not to know what had already been carefully explained to her?

A third important area was in helping them to take steps towards some separation. Holly had had a catastrophic early separation from home. When she was 4 years old, she had been placed in a psychiatric hospital at a distance from home for almost a year, spending only weekends with her family. Her mother understood deeply that this had been severely traumatic for Holly. In fact, ultimately the mother had refused to take her back because the weekly separations had been so unbearably painful. Her guilt about this enforced early separation made any move towards thinking of Holly leaving home very difficult. This arose first in discussion of schooling. When I first met her, Holly was going to a local school for learning-disabled children. This was profoundly unsuitable—she was driving the teachers crazy with her loud psychotic chatter throughout the day, and she was being actively abused by other children in the playground, who were frightened of her madness and dealt with this by exploiting and degrading her. A change of school meant a long journey and, ultimately, a weekly boarding arrangement, with weekends at home. Holly and her mother shared a sense of impending catastrophe about this—her mother felt that she would never be forgiven for a second separation, and Holly believed that she was being confined to a torture chamber for a second time. However, by moving a step at a time, each of them was released from their timeless convictions so that reality could impinge, and the shift took place. Later this had to be reworked when, at the age of 19, the only possible placement for further education and development acceptable to the parents involved Holly going to live in a community 40 miles away, where the expectation was that residents spent a good many weekends within the community. My capacity to defend the continuity of Holly's therapy over these changes seemed to help her mother believe that all would not be lost.

The final area of work I want to comment on only took shape in the last two years of Holly's therapy, and I believe it came about once we had begun to think together about when her treatment would end. Her mother began to use the sessions to share with her husband for the first time some of her own terrible family history. He had always known of Holly's mother's older institutionalized schizophrenic sister—she, indeed, was the maternal grandmother's model of Holly's future unless everyone protected her by entering her mad world. What he had never known was that Holly's mother's stepfather—her own father having died when she was very young—was a paranoid schizophrenic who had terrified both his wife and her two daughters by his violent unpredictable outbursts. Mother's childhood had thus been lived in the shadow of a psychotic sister and a psychotic father figure. As I learnt this, I was deeply impressed by the bravery with which this woman had fought and was fighting for access to an ordinary non-mad world. Something that she had found in our work helped her in this life-long struggle and also enabled her to reach a new level of trust in her husband's love and solidity.

It may be useful to add two small technical notes. I found that I needed to allow 75 minutes for the meetings with this couple. To give adequate attention both to issues concerning Holly and to the unfolding of their own personalities was not possible within the 50-minute frame. Even then, it was usually very difficult to end sessions, though the father became able to help me by remaining aware of the passing of time, and gradually the mother too gained a sense of the structure of the session and could gather herself together to be ready to leave. She was often almost overwhelmed by emotion during the session, yet dignified in her effort to regain some composure with which to depart. The second point is that the mother was free to telephone me in between our appointments. She was respectful of this in not making very frequent calls, but it was difficult to manage the length of conversations when she did ring. She did so when she was very worried about an impending external change and its impact on Holly, and also when she felt that she must tell me about a change in Holly that she knew was significant but could not herself understand. Touchingly, she rang me the week after Holly's final session to tell me that Holly was sad, that they had talked about it, and that Holly had said to her, "I want to be in that room so that I can talk to Mrs Rustin". Mother was both afraid that Holly would not manage without me and also moved by Holly's lucid search for support from her.

Third clinical example

Now I shall go on to describe a second model for this support-ive work with parents. (I am indebted to Judith Loose for this clinical material).

Mr and Mrs B, parents of a young autistic girl, "Beth", were seen weekly together in parallel with their daughter's treatment. For a long time, their worker felt defeated by the repetitive, ruminative, anxious flow of talk from Mrs B which would lead to Mr B's eyes glazing over and his withdrawal from involvement.

Mrs B lost her mother when she was a few months old. She had a poor relationship with her stepmother and hates her half-sister, who is severely mentally ill. Mr B came to England after traumatizing war service.

The therapist found herself unable to imagine how this couple could have had children, as they seemed so disconnected. In the early part of a session taking place after about one year of treatment, there had been a lively moment sparked off by Mrs B's tart observation that their therapist had not taken half-terms last year but was doing so this term. Mr B had spoken of the misdiagnosis of a serious illness of his father's, and his belief that it was best to steer clear of doctors who make mistakes but lack humility. Mrs B had criticized the school's failure to provide Beth with clean pants after an accident—she had been sent home in a nappy. "If they have spare nappies, why not spare pants?" There was reference to a happy family outing, and talk of Beth's new capacity for discrimination about food. Then the session continued with the therapist enquiring of Mrs B about her memories of family meals.

Mrs B said sadly that her main meal was school lunch. Because her father came home late, she had tea either with what would have been called today a child minder or, after her father remarried, with her stepmother and her younger sister who was just a baby. This last part was said with some coldness. The therapist asked about snacks. What did she do when she was hungry? She seemed grateful to be asked and told an amusing story of not being allowed to eat sweets when wearing school uniform. Mr B looked interested, as if he had never heard this story. Mum acknowledged how different it was today for Alice, their older daughter, who bought crisps whenever she felt like it.

When Mr B was asked if he remembered childhood meals, he said with a smile that they were big ones, especially breakfast, and the family was all together, often including a grandparent. He seemed momentarily happy and continued talking about high school and university, when he had had jobs on farms to earn extra money. He said that then he had eaten with the farm families. He mentioned that city jobs were hard to come by, but he could always find work "defoliating" once he had a good reputation. The therapist asked if he could explain "defoliating".

He seemed to come alive. He described the process of corn hybrids and pollination rows in an almost passionate way. He spoke about walking up and down the countless rows with a kind of rhythm, pulling back the husk leaves of each individual corn. Mrs B actually turned in her chair so that she was facing him for the first time ever. The therapist felt no need to hold onto the details as he had been able to capture his wife's attention. She was looking at him with surprising warmth.

Discussion

I think that this material brings out very beautifully a process taking place between these parents, which is being presided over by their therapist. Husband and wife are becoming interested in each other's separate existence—time spent apart in past or present is felt to be enriching their relationship. The primitive deprivation and neediness within this mother is less oppressive. The session seems to be giving them pleasure.

The technique that the therapist had adopted to counter the mindless flow of words that had engulfed earlier sessions has three elements, all rooted in meticulous observation. First, the therapist is quick to pick up the negative transference. She shows herself to have strength to deal with this, and this modifies Mrs B's infantile despair about being attended to, a consequence of the early loss of her mother and her feeling of having been too much for her mother. There is some introjective identification with a competent adult in Mr and Mrs B's belated efforts to toilet-train

Beth. Second, the therapist interrupts Mrs B when repetitive stories appear, in an effort to hold Mr B's interest and to convey that Mrs B can be contained and that Mr B's active presence in the sessions is valued. Third, she expresses active interest in and curiosity about the thoughts and feelings of each of the parents. This gives the message of the importance of their different life stories and of the possibility of an enriched conversation when each person can be listened to. Once the therapist had allowed herself to become more actively curious, she was enabled to discover that Beth had been sleeping in her parents' room up to this point. Following some discussion of this, Mrs B reported a family weekend away when she had made up an extension bed next to theirs in the holiday hotel but noticed that Beth wanted to look at the twin bed next to Alice's. Mother had taken the point of this. This enquiring attitude of the therapist requires that care is taken to achieve a clear understanding—when she does not understand, she persists. This counters the tendency within families with an autistic member for experience of clear and rewarding communication to atrophy and for misunderstandings to abound. Mr B makes an implicit comparison between his experience of this therapist, who knows what she is doing, and earlier experience of doctors that had been so unsatisfactory.

I think that as child psychotherapists we are well suited to do the kind of work just described (Barrows, 1995). Our attunement to the infantile in our patients allows us access to the disturbance in adult and parental functioning which needs to be addressed. This case is an example of work where our own parental aspects—of taking responsibility for protecting vulnerability, for challenging self-destructive behaviour, for interesting ourselves in the every-day details of children's lives—are called upon. Such work may serve to give a first experience to deprived adults of attentive and thoughtful parental behaviour.

Work to promote change in family functioning

Now I shall move to discuss the cluster of cases where there is an agreed explicit aim of change within the family. This might lead to marital therapy or family therapy as such, but I would like to note one kind of work which, I think, appropriately attracts child psychotherapists. This is individual psychotherapeutic work with a parent, where there is a particular emphasis on clarifying the projections occurring between family members. This can be seen as analogous in some ways to psychoanalytically based family therapy (Copley, 1987). Such work makes use of transference in the therapeutic relationship, but the emphasis is more firmly focused on exploring the transferences within the family, with the aim of improving emotional containment. This can free the parent to function in a parental mode and the child to be less burdened with intergenerational difficulties.

Fourth clinical example

My work with Miss C, a single mother who had adopted "John" at the age of 6 years, began when John was 14. Mother and son had been seen together from time to time by the child psychiatrist who had been involved in the original adoption placement. In early adolescence, John became very angry and upset. He was doing badly at school, increasingly involved with delinquent gang-life and drug culture, and out of control at home. He was extremely abusive to his mother and stole from her on a large scale.

My psychiatrist colleague asked me to see Miss C while she continued with John, following an episode when he smashed a picture in an explosion of rage during a joint session. The initial nine months were a time of real turbulence. John was admitted to an adolescent in-patient unit for a while, and his mother was desperate and frightened much of the time. She gradually became able to reassert her authority, gained support when needed from the local police, and came to understand that she could not allow John to live at home if he persisted in theft from and violence towards her. Eventually he was housed in an excellent hostel with a key-worker support system.

I shall present some recent material that is characteristic of the mix of themes tackled in this once-weekly work. Miss C is an unusual person. She is an intelligent and imaginative woman with many gifts, but there have been great impediments in her making use of these in her life. Her history is important in understanding this. She is the child of German Jewish refugees who escaped from Berlin in 1938. Many of their relatives died in the Holocaust. She had one brother who died in his early 30s. She has not married, although she has had some very close relationships with men, and she has many friends.

After some months of crisis-driven work, it became clear to me that she needed psychotherapy in her own right. I talked to her about this, making it clear that this would be a different experience from what had happened so far, and adding that she might like me to refer her to a separate service, since the Child and Family Department might feel like a place for her and John together, but that, if she wished, I would be able to work with her on this basis, since we had already come to understand a good deal together. We agreed to end our weekly meetings, leaving her two months in which she could think this over. My vacancy would be available from the following term if she decided to take it up.

She accepted my offer, though giving me a taste of what was to come by falling violently in love on a trip abroad, which entailed cancelling our first two sessions of the term.

John is now 18. Miss C had an accident last December in which she broke her leg badly. She had to miss the last session before Christmas, and most of those during January, because she was immobilized. She then returned on two crutches. It was clear to both of us that this accident was linked to beginning to think about the end of therapy—the fall was a consequence of her missing the last step on the stairs and seemed to represent her anxiety that facing the end was a time of danger for her, of not feeling safely held inside.

In the session I want to refer to, she began by noticing that in the sink in my room, the name "John" is engraved in metal (the sink-maker's trademark). She smiled and said he might not like that. She went on to describe her journey to my room and her thought as she struggled along the corridor: "I don't want to be a patient any more, not at the Tavistock or the Whittington [a local hospital]". She felt she would never get to the first floor and could not bear her dependence on the lift, on the reception-ist to tell me she was here, on the woman who did not help her by holding the swing doors, or on me who decided when she could come. She was feeling very wobbly, she added.

I linked this to our recognition that the end of her therapy was now going to be talked about between us, leaving her in a rush to get away, and yet wobbly and needy. She went on to talk about John, who is serving a six-week prison sentence. She had been very worried about him this week, knowing that his phone calls were leaving something out. Eventually he told her that he had been in a fight and had been locked up in solitary confinement for a week. She movingly described the circum-stances: he had been reading ("You'll never believe this, Mum", he told her) and had been taunted by a group of young men, and this ended up in fighting. He said it had been awful, but he had coped. He had a long talk with the governor, who said that he was not the sort of young man who should be in prison. She spoke of his negotiating to have some unpaid fines dealt with as part of his prison sentence, so that he can start with a clean slate when he came out. "John is so balanced, in the way he is trying to work this out", she said, and she grinned as she thought of her own huge efforts to keep her balance. "I offered to help him with the fines and said I did not want him to be in prison longer, but he wrote to me that he wanted to sort it out himself and that it would be all right. But somehow he thinks I have the key." I spoke about her confusion—she wishes to be in my mind, engraved there like John's name on my sink, but then gets frightened that I will not let her go, might imprison her. She finds it so difficult to believe that, when she feels me to be a mother who needs to hold on to her, she can also find a father-aspect of me who might help her to feel ready to leave. I talked at some length about the idea of being held in my mind as a living separate being who would end her therapy here and go on to live her life as I would my own.

She went on to talk about her fatherless nephew, for whom she often provides counsel; the theme of finding father's voice was explored in relation to John and to her nephew, and in the transference, and she then talked about her own father's role in supporting her during her university years. "But later on he couldn't help me", she mused. To her own amazement she found herself recalling sitting at a café frequented by German refugees where she would meet her father when she came to live and work in London. He brought a book to show her, Victor Zorza's account of his daughter's death from cancer. She spoke movingly of her parents' complete inability to talk to each other about their son's illness and death, and of her father describing to her the comfort of reading this book and asking her to read it too, but never to speak to her mother about it.

Later she connected this unshared and incomplete mourning with the recent funeral of an aunt, and her nephew's wish to visit his father's grave, and for the headstone to be altered to include him.

I described her longing to bring together the strong father-aspect of me with whom she felt that these tragedies—like those of the refugees in the café—could be shared and the mother-aspect, to confront the idea that she always had to take a protective role towards me and not speak of her wish to end therapy and leave me. I linked this to her pre-Christmas accident and showed her that she feels that it is very dangerous to herself to live in accordance with this belief. I described her hope that she could encounter in me a sense of mother and father in communication with each other.

The session ended with her speaking of how after her aunt's death she had talked for the first time to her mother about all the family members who died in the camps. She found out that her mother did know their names and where they had been killed and buried. A friend going to Auschwitz recently had sought out their names and said Kaddish for them.

She said, "I came back here to find a different way to leave", and I agreed that this was so. I had myself been feeling during her January absence that helping her to get back so that an ending could take place was going to be a difficult task.

This material is much condensed, but I think that it does illustrate what I mean about the multilayered work that we can sometimes do in working with parents. Despite John's continuing difficulties, the two of them have re-established a real relationship. When he heard of her accident, he came rushing to the hospital at once, and in a recent letter from prison he said that he had realized that she was not only a good mum, but also a good friend to him. Her part in this great change has been to struggle with huge personal difficulties in establishing a separate identity, to give up a predominantly manic defensive system, and to sort out the unmourned dead (who haunted her dreams) from the child adopted in part because he represented the necessity to rescue the abandoned Jews who had not escaped. Inevitably, the details of her family story revealed a terrible toll of guilt. This work has left a space in which she and her son have begun to get to know each other in a fresh way.

Referral outside the child and family setting

Sometimes we find ourselves referring a parent with major difficulties to an adult psychotherapist or analyst outside the child and family psychiatric setting. One of the disadvantages of this is that there may be rather little attention paid to the damaging projective processes going on in the family in the present. Within the Tavistock, we have found that referrals to the adult department for psychotherapy of a parent sometimes create a painful split between the priority given to the infantile needs of the patient and the protection required for vulnerable children and young people. When an adult patient is being seen within an adult psychotherapy service, the attention paid to the impact of the patient's internal difficulties on parental functioning is less to the fore. Psychotherapy provided within the child and family setting, and by therapists with experience of work with children, tends to be particularly attuned to the interferences in adult relational capacities which are consequent on infantile anxieties and phantasies, and to concentrate on delineating and differentiating adult from infantile aspects of the personality (Harris, 1970). This approach, which depends on a firm gathering of the infantile transference within the therapy, is supportive of improved parental functioning.

Ethical issues

Finally, I should like to share a few reflections on ethical issues raised in work with parents. There are two areas of concern: one is when there is a refusal on the part of parents to take their children's welfare seriously; the second is where therapy with the parent may endanger their capacity to sustain adult functioning.

When we are faced with clear cases of abuse of children, we can usually resolve how to proceed, although the limited resources of social services and the clumsiness of the law can be a troubling disincentive. More tricky are examples of emotional abuse. A case in point would be the following.

Fifth clinical example

I found myself working with a couple—well known in the local community as public figures—in relation to the therapy of their adopted son, "Robert". Robert was failing at school and stole things at home. He denied these acts of theft resolutely. In his therapy, there was soon a defensive impasse. In my work with the couple I learnt that the father (a magistrate) was black-mailing the mother not to speak about problems in the family relationships—his sanction was to absent himself from our meetings and thereafter to withdraw support for the child's therapy. On one occasion, they brought a small model made by Robert, who was very good at art. It was a highly disturbing devil figure, clearly related to father's looks. The father demon-strated his pride in his son's technical capacity—and his lack of awareness of the reference to himself—and then proceeded to use the model as evidence that his son would go to the bad. He took the devil image as concrete evidence of the "bad blood" that the child had inherited from his aberrant natural parents. The cold rejection and lack of concern for the boy's future in his attitude was breathtaking. In due course, I learnt from the mother, who returned in a more desperate state some time after the ending of Robert's unsatisfactory therapy, that the family was based on a profound lie—the father was carrying on a secret affair with a woman on the staff of the court and denying the truth of this when she confronted him. He was, in fact, as determined a liar as Robert.

The work it was possible to do was very limited. The mother was too frightened of the loss of her social position and relative economic security to force the issue with her husband. Meanwhile, the corrosive effects of this hypocritical situation on the children were serious. Robert's delinquent behaviour had escalated; his father's attitude combined cynical despair with vicarious enjoyment of Robert's dangerous lifestyle. I tried to help the mother to take seriously the price being paid for the maintenance of this dishonest structure, and she pulled herself out of some of her self-destructive, collusive behaviour.

Sixth clinical example

A different kind of ethical issue arises when we are faced with a parent at risk of breakdown. A recent case illustrates this well. (I am grateful to Biddy Youell for this material.)

Mrs D is an experienced foster-mother. She was being seen once a week at the clinic to support her in the care of two very seriously abused children and to sustain her commitment to bringing them to therapy. The children are aged 8 and 6 years.

The crisis I want to describe occurred following Mrs D's decision to adopt the children. She took them to visit her mother and brother in New Zealand over Christmas and returned saying that she could no longer cope with their difficult behaviour and wanted them removed. Social services were horrified, as Mrs D had been seen as a tower of strength who could cope with anything. They offered extra support but also told Mrs D that if she could not cope, then the children would have to go into institutional care. This made her feel very guilty. The social services department was in a panic because these children had been abused both sexually and physically while in care, in two previous foster homes. This had led to court cases, and several social workers had been disciplined for negligence.

Mrs D's therapist found herself struggling with very painful, conflicting questions. The children's therapist as well as social services wanted Mrs D to be persuaded to hold on to them. But Mrs D's therapist had before her a woman in a state of extreme emotional collapse, beneath the façade of rejection and blame of the children. Their behaviour had regressed while they were on holiday, and her relatives had been disgusted by them. Quite soon, Mrs D acknowledged that she knew she was ill. She shivered, hunched in silent tears, and spoke of how she felt unable to take the antidepressants prescribed by her GP for fear that the pills would take away her last vestiges of control. She feared falling into the state of mind of the time when she was widowed. She described nightmares of hundreds of worms, and of driving into a black hole.

The therapist was aware that Mrs D had been a "coper" all her life. She had found a solution to her own early deprivation in becoming a super-competent carer. This identity had collapsed, and it was evident that she could not care for the children at this point. The painful question was how to maintain proper concern for her mental health. She needed some protection from the demands of child care professionals who could not bear her breakdown. Additionally, the therapist felt anxious that her weekly supportive work with Mrs D might have contributed to her becoming more open to her fragile underlying emotional state and have undermined her very rigid defences.

This case therefore raised the issue of our judgement about when defences need to be supported—for example, might it have been wiser to accept Mrs D's initial assertion that once-monthly sessions would be fine for her? When we work with parents who are themselves very deprived or have other borderline features, keeping the temperature of the involvement cool may sometimes be wise. The support systems we build for our work with adults are one of the crucial elements in giving us a sense of proper professional authority.

Conclusion

People who want to train and work as child psychotherapists usually have a profound identification with the child's point of view. This perspective provides us with ready access to the child aspects of our adult patients' personalities. When there is an opportunity to do psychotherapeutic work using the infantile transference, we have rich experience to draw on. This has to be married with an awareness of other issues in adult lives, and in adult psychotherapy. Nonetheless, the intensive training in psychoanalytic work with children and young people provides a very strong base from which to tackle this work. The passionate conflicts of family life are what bring parents to seek our help, and often the pain opened up by troubles between parents and children provides an appropriate opening for facing fundamental issues. We sometimes have an exceptional opportunity to help and need to have the confidence to do so.

CHAPTER TWO

Therapeutic space for re-creating the child in the mind of the parents

Viviane Green

A t The Anna Freud Centre, work with parents takes place in many different ways and in many different contexts. Outside the immediate classical therapeutic context, parents can be seen in educational or health settings, as, for example, the nursery setting at The Anna Freud Centre. Work with parents is also carried out in the Parent Infant Project and the Parent Support Project. This chapter does not represent the entire range of work carried out at the Centre. For the purposes of this chapter, which is based on group discussions at the Centre, I have focused on work with parents in conjunction with a child's therapy or as a prelude to therapy.

Parents can be seen primarily to support and hold a child's analysis. Sometimes the child is worked with through the parents. At other times, parents work actively with a therapist in parallel

A paper on which this chapter is based was presented at the Annual Conference of the Association of Child Psychotherapists in March 1997. It was based on group discussions, and I am extremely grateful to my colleagues at The Anna Freud Centre for contributing to many of the ideas and for offering vignettes.

with their child's treatment. Through accident rather than design, the vignettes selected were all of cases where the child's therapist also worked with the parents; usually, however, the parents will be seen by a social worker or another therapist. In this chapter, I hope to show that, whilst there may be several themes that arise commonly in work with many parents, ultimately the clinical starting point for the worker is defined by the locus of the parent.

Forming an alliance with the parents

Several therapists have expressed the view that there is something inherent in the state of parenthood itself that can make people psychically open to change. The literature has many examples about the nature and extent of capacity for change that is wrought in the wake of being a parent. In moving and passionate language, Selma Fraiberg (1980) expressed what can lie on the side of hope: "The baby (though this could be extended to include the child) can be a catalyst. He provides a powerful motive for positive changes in his parents. He represents their hopes and deepest longings: he stands for renewal of the self: his birth can be experienced as a psychological rebirth for his parents" (pp. 53–54). In this state of more available experiential fluidity, the mother, through her response to her child, can begin to explore what her child means to her and how those meanings link into relevant and often painful aspects of her own history, allowing for a new internal accommodation not just to her own history but to her child.

Children can generate and offer a reparative hope in their parents who wish to parent in a better way than they feel they were parented. Whilst this may, of course, produce the opposite effect, it does seem important that the *wish* to be a good-enough parent is there and that this feeds into the therapeutic alliance. There can thus be many forces to assist us operating within parents themselves.

Nevertheless, manifest positive motivations can also co-exist with latent unconscious "destructive" wishes, feelings, and impulses. These, too, need to be taken into account, particularly when assessing the parents' capacity to nurture and support treatment for their child. Overall, there needs to be sufficient parental investment in the progressive aspects of their child's development. If the unconscious wish or need is to have a symptomatic, developmentally regressed or even "stuck" child, it will be extremely hard for the parents to support their child's forward moves and therapy is likely to be sabotaged.

Our discussion group focused on parent work in relation to a child's therapy. We wondered whether parents were sufficiently considered in the initial assessment for therapy. By this I mean not simply whether they would agree to a recommendation for analysis or therapy, but what part they could or would play in the process of change. We asked ourselves what, more specifically, we needed to bear in mind when trying to think about the parents, their capacities for engagement, and the type of work in which they could be engaged.

In trying to understand parenthood itself, perhaps a distinction needs to be made between the parental aspect of the adult personality and the rest of the adult's functioning. There are adults who, despite manifest difficulties in other areas of their lives, are nonetheless excellent parents. Conversely, there are those who function very well in their work and adult relationships but find parenting very difficult. Parenthood is a developmental stage within the life of an adult. When assessing parents, Furman (1966) suggests that we seek to establish whether either or both have entered the developmental phase of parenthood. "To what extent," she asks, "have they have been able to maintain and progress in their development relative to the child's growth?" The accent is placed somewhat differently by Daniel Stern (1995) when he writes about motherhood as a constellation of affective and psychic capacities which can be activated at any point in a mother's life. However, he too views motherhood in developmental terms, delineating the gradual, necessary shift in the mother from the infant–mother constellation, moving into the later oedipal constellation. He stresses that mothers have a special need to feel valued, supported, aided, guided, and appreciated by a maternal figure. When sufficiently "held" in this way, a mother's own maternal functions are discovered and facilitated.

Both these views conceive of parenthood as a *dynamic* state open to change and the activation of capacities. This creates room for seeing the enormous variation and fluctuations not only between parents as to how they experience their state, but within one parent at different points in his or her parental development. This variability would suggest that the ways in which we as therapists need to work with parents will be diverse and will require great flexibility on our part.

A toddler requires rather different parenting from that of an adolescent. Different capacities are called forth in parents throughout the child's development, in line with the child's phase-specific needs. In relation to this, I was put in mind of the now "popular" notion of the child's development of a theory of mind. This phraseology refers to the complex series of affective and cognitive processes that unfold in the course of good-enough development, whereby the child, through having had sufficient experiences of a caretaking adult's attunement to and mirroring of his states of mind and feeling, gradually becomes able to attribute separate thoughts/minds and states to himself and others. In a way, I wondered if parenting could be thought of as involving a continuing equivalent process, a parental reflective function. By this I mean an ongoing process of refinement and revision of the parents' theories of mind about their children congruent with and in response to their child's level of development.

A further consideration is the parents' capacity for emotional awareness of their child as not only a dependent and connected person, but also a developing and separate one, with a shifting balance between the two. I found it interesting to see how this idea dressed itself in different conceptual and linguistic apparel. In terms of more classical theory it is described as a shift in the balance of the parents' narcissistic economy. Erna Furman (1966) expressed it as follows: "Functioning with and for each other is the necessary outcome of the special investment parents and children have in one another. I characterised the parents' entry into the developmental phase of parenthood by their ability to invest their child both as a loved person and as a part of themselves" (p. 25). The necessary investment in the infant and child as a part of the self is termed narcissistic, whereas the love for the child in its own right is termed object love. The balance between the two alters as the child grows and develops.

An additional way of trying to gauge how far a child can be empathically thought of and understood in his own right is to get a sense of the role that he fulfils within the family and in relation to each of the parents. What projections does the child have to carry, and what or whom do they represent for and to the parents? Indeed, therapeutic work often entails setting in motion processes of disentanglement. At one end of the continuum will be the parents who, for perhaps pathological reasons of their own (such as entrenched narcissistic difficulties), find it very hard to view their child as separate from their own needs and desires. Somewhere else along the continuum might be the parents who struggle beyond their own anger, fear, hurt, or disappointment to understand their child but nonetheless find themselves constrained by their own histories, limitations, or conflicts. At the most hopeful end are those parents who are readily able to be emotionally aware of their child's feelings.

The broad aim of work with parents (alongside seeing them through the vicissitudes of their child's treatment) is to engage them in an unfolding process in which their child could gradually be understood and responded to in his or her own right. Often this can only begin after the establishment of a background of safety and through acknowledging the parents' guilt and shame. In several of the clinical vignettes below, the work could shift into a different key only when the mother or father had felt safe enough to take ownership of his or her own superego conflicts, with a corresponding easing up of criticism of their child. The narcissistic hurt of having a child in need of help also required careful attention with almost all parents.

The admittedly rather non-specific idea of working with the parents to understand and respond to their child seemed to exist as a therapeutic ideal because, in fact, we are often faced with the question of how to work with the variety of difficulties that parents presented that constrained their capacity to understand and respond appropriately to their children. Often, the initial phase of working with parents entails working towards the point where they can awaken their emotional awareness of their child and begin to reflect on their relationship.

The child in the parents' mind

When engaged with parents, we begin to get a qualitative sense of two related themes:

1. In what way does a parent hold her child in mind?
2. What sort of child is harboured in the parent's mind?

With regard to the parent's cathexis of a child, the capacity to hold a child in mind is not an absolute state or capacity. In some parents, there is an affective and attentional capacity to be mindful of their child consistently and protractedly. In others, where the parents' own defences or internal preoccupations consume their psychic energies, "mindfulness" fluctuates. The child might be held in mind up until such point where something about the child impinges on an internal difficulty in the parent. In a few parents, there could be intermittent decathexis of their child, particularly as a result of parental depression.

Of course the child, as he exists in the parents' mind, might be a rather opaque being, brought alive in the parental imagination through the forces of the parents' own internal sense of their histories, conflicts, fears, needs, and wishes. However, the precise constellation of difficulties that accrue around and obscure the child varies widely. Each parent is starting at a different point. In addition to this, therapists have rather different ways of connecting to parents and understanding how change, where it occurs, is wrought.

The child and parents in the therapist's mind

Work with parents in parallel to a child's treatment raises many questions about our own therapeutic stance; in particular, where do we situate ourselves psychically *vis-à-vis* the mother and/or father and child? The child's dependence on his parents for emotional and physical growth distinguishes child therapy from work with adults. The primacy of the parent–child relationship needs to be held in the therapist's mind, and the therapeutic attitude needs to be imbued with a profound respect for that relationship in its complex mutuality.

Much of this may seem self-evident, but attempting to keep equidistant from both the parent and the child at the level of thinking, whilst at the same time allowing oneself full affective freedom to experience a whole range of feelings from empathy to being infuriated by one or the other party, is one of the real difficulties in this work, particularly where the therapist works with both parties. At times, it is hard to avoid finding oneself sliding into a position of identifying with just one or the other side. One can also experience a pressure to become an advocate, usually of the child.

Keeping the parent/child couple or triad alive in the therapist's mind also means recognizing the particular quality of the investment the parents have in their children and its profound and inextricable tie to their own narcissism. In all the cases cited, the therapist had to acknowledge the extent of parents' guilt and sometimes visceral hurt at recognizing that their child is in need.

The use of the transference and countertransference

The therapist endeavours to restore the "real" child in the parental mind by attempting to engage the parents in the process of empathic understanding. In direct relation to this, a recurrent theme is the therapist's use of the transference and countertransference, the raw material informing her insights. Several ways of working with the transference and countertransference were explored in the discussion group. With some parents, explicit use of the transference and countertransference can be made from the outset. At other times, parent work involves working in the positive transference by offering oneself as a new parental developmental object. This means not working exclusively in the positive transference but annexing the positive forces in the transference for the specific purpose of creating the conditions for a sense of safety within the parents, thereby ushering in a process of identification with and internalization of the therapist as a reactivated or new developmental object. Through this integrative process, parents are then enabled to animate their own capacity for reflection on their child.

In one of the examples below, it was only after the parent experienced her therapist as a sufficiently benign presence that she could allow herself to become aware of how critical she was towards herself and, by extension, her child. A further view was that in some instances, whilst transference and countertransference communications are implicitly understood by the therapist, they are not necessarily always alluded to either directly or obliquely and do not necessarily lead to interpretations as in individual therapy. These different possibilities are by no means mutually exclusive, but highlight the therapeutic sensitivity needed as regards the rhythms, timing, and "cadences" in the work and acknowledge that work with parents goes through different phases.

Clinical vignettes

In the following clinical vignettes I hope to illustrate how some of these issues reveal themselves in clinical practice. The vignettes explore the germane themes of the nature of the parents' difficulties and how these impacted on the type of internal picture they created of their child. Technical questions about ways of working within the transference and the countertransference are embedded in the vignettes.

Vignette 1

The first vignette illustrates brief work with parents where the focus was towards accepting analysis for their child. In this case, the therapist was keenly aware that the child's symptomatology embodied an entanglement in the parents' own difficulties and projections. The parents would first need to see past their projections and mutually recriminatory guilt before they could more fully perceive and acknowledge their child's pain and consequent need for help.

The therapist was contacted by Mrs E regarding their 9-year-old daughter, "Sophie", who was unhappy and enuretic. Previous contact with professionals had not been followed through.

During the first interview with Mr and Mrs E, an argument developed between them over their daughter Sophie's bedwetting. Mrs E said that the enuresis was a sign of unhappiness, whereas Mr E thought that Sophie's misery was the effect of her enuresis. What emerged, after the therapist invited their further thoughts, was an intergenerational link when Mr E disclosed how he, too, had been a miserable enuretic child. Mr E and the therapist spoke about his experiences at length, with the therapist displaying her sympathy to his pain as a youngster. Eventually, the therapist suggested that perhaps Mr E found his daughter's symptom particularly difficult as it reminded him of an aspect of himself that he did not like—that is, his own lack of "control". The therapist did not leave it there but related it to the present home situation, in which he often berated his daughter about her bedwetting. Interestingly, Mr E had made a link to his own past, and in taking it up the therapist integrated his past with his current response. The therapist remarked that perhaps in making comments to his daughter he was seeking to control what he had been unable to control in himself. This integration leaves open the links to the past but underscores its significance in the present and in relation to the child. It is this bringing into awareness of how Mr E was driven to treat his child that seems important and specific to work with these parents. In response to the therapist's remark, Mr E then added that he would try to stop making derogatory remarks to Sophie as it made her feel bad. In her parting sentence, Mrs E informed the therapist that she did not feel safe at home because of her husband's volatile temper.

Following two sessions with Sophie, the therapist met with the parents to give them some feedback. The focus was on her deep unhappiness. In what followed, the therapist had not only to grasp the family dynamics and identifications that contributed to Sophie's unhappiness, but to recognize and use her own countertransferential sense of feeling unsafe. Mrs E described how Sophie was bullied by her older sister. This led Mr E to disagree, saying that she brought it on herself, thus displaying his own investment and identification with his bullying daughter. The therapist used this to remark how difficult it was when even home did not feel safe. The parents began to argue and blame each other, and the therapist was aware that father was the primary bully. The therapist eventually directly acknowledged the mother's remarks from the previous session about her own feelings of lack of safety. At the same time, the therapist was aware that Mrs E was angry with her. The therapist had come to represent the "bad" object because of Mrs E's projected guilt about her daughter's unhappiness. The therapist took up her possible upset, which was confirmed when the mother's parting shot was her dissatisfaction that the therapist had not told them what would be helpful for Sophie.

In the next session, Mr E reported that he had announced to the children that bullying would not be tolerated and offered to help his daughter when she felt bullied by her sister. Mr E then found himself on the receiving end of his daughter's hatred. The therapist said that it must be very painful for him and that Sophie knew how to hurt as much as she felt hurt. Here, the therapist made the active suggestion that her father could respond to her by conveying that he would remain her father no matter how much she hated him at times, thus enabling him to reclaim his parental position of loving his unhappy and hating daughter.

The therapist then went on to make her recommendation for intensive treatment for Sophie, citing her age, the intensity of her unhappiness, and her symptomatology as the reasons. The implications of psychoanalysis as opposed to other approaches was explored, as well as the need for a secure set-up supported by the parents. Here, the previous failed attempts were discussed. The other half of the therapist's two-pronged approach was that the parents would be offered regular meetings to discuss issues they wanted to raise.

In the ensuing session, Mrs E's ambivalence came up. In part, there was a realistic questioning of psychoanalysis and of the qualifications that the person would bring to the work. In part, there seemed to be a potential for Mrs E to destroy Sophie's relationship with a therapist, as expressed in her question: "Would the therapist know what to do if, for instance, Sophie proved resistant to coming?" They talked through these issues, and the therapist added that the mother was also conveying her pain about having an unhappy daughter and her sense that perhaps something she or her husband had done made it hard for Sophie's development. This time, instead of blaming her husband, the mother wondered what it was that she had not done, then turned to her husband and acknowledged that perhaps they, too, needed to go for help.

In this rather fraught family, the parent work had to be undertaken before Sophie could be offered help. The skill seemed to lie in knowing how to transform the raw feeling of hostility between the parents and the impact of the "fallout" on the therapist into a communication that could be taken in by the parents. An ongoing question left for this particular therapist was: how much pathology do you take up in parent work?

In this work, there was a shifting focus from the child to the parents and back. However, where the ghosts in the parents' own pathology came to haunt their relationships with their daughter, the therapist gave room for the "historical" link but repeatedly brought this back to the present situation. I do not wish to suggest that parent work takes place only in the present in relation to the child, nor to counterpose this to adult psychotherapy as the place where further exploration of the past would be invited. Rather, I wish simply to throw open for consideration whether there are stages in work with parents where one might focus more on the present than the past or, indeed, vice versa.

Vignette 2

The next vignette touches on several of the themes mentioned earlier, in particular the parents' guilt, hurt, and shame at having a child in need of help. The child who existed in his parents' mind was a diminished boy, defined mainly in terms of his oddities and irritation to others. Given Mr and Mrs F's limited possibilities for reflection, the therapist wondered if change could come about in other ways.

Mr and Mrs F felt narcissistically hurt, guilty, and bewilderedly disappointed at having a visibly odd/damaged son. In turn this gave rise to extremes of hope or despair about his progress. The therapist's struggle was to work with the parents in a way that would allow a more connected and realistic view of their son. The challenge was how to help effect affective change in the parents who had no capacity to readily understand their child. Here, the therapist felt that the main thrust of her work was through the parents' identification with the therapist's *attitude* towards their child.

"Martin" entered into analytic treatment at 7 years 4 months. His father had given many examples of his bizarre behaviour, his difficulties in understanding the spoken word, and his refusal to participate in group activities. At school, he was the subject of derision. The child's therapist also worked with the parents. Mother and father attended together until work commitments made this impossible, and they were then seen individually. The therapist struggled in juggling with her complex feelings towards the parents. Through her own direct experience of Martin, she could understand and acknowledge their hurt and frustration with their demanding child. This was tempered by her irritation with their difficulty in thinking about his particular needs, which ran counter to her own empathy for the child and understanding. She had to work with the parents to create a space not simply to think about their child's special needs, which involved holding in mind a balanced recognition of his strengths and limitations, but also to enable them to view their son in a way that tapped into their potential to enjoy him tenderly and patiently, without overwhelming and unrealistic expectations. In brief, it was to work towards an affective shift in the parents.

The parents were both high achievers. Mrs F had remained at home for the first five years of Martin's life. From early on, Martin's development was erratic. He had periods of ill health and deafness until he was 5 years old. His speech did not develop normally. This influenced ego functions such as synthesis, reality testing, and secondary-process thinking. Both parents had very limited psychological awareness, and Martin's difficulties were intensified by their inability to give meaning to his feeling states. Nonetheless, they were conscientious parents who grew to trust the help Martin received.

The therapist described the mother as without psychological awareness, and working with her was experienced as rather taxing. Mrs F tended to deny the extent of her son's difficulties and hoped that they would eventually disappear. The main focus of the work took place at the level of Mrs F's identification with the therapist's feeling that Martin was worthwhile, endearing, and commendably motivated to mastery. Through this identification, Mrs F was able to allow herself to experience a tenderness and compassion that tempered the hurt guilt and irritation.

Mr F was an apparently gentle, sensitive man. He was very pessimistic about Martin's future and critical of his regressive behaviours. In his sessions, his anxiety was often expressed in the form of complaints and disgust about, for example, Martin's table manners. His intense disappointment in his son blinded him to Martin's yearning for his father's approval. The therapist actively experienced Martin's frustration at their unwitting insensitivity and, simultaneously, the parents' pain over his present and future predicament.

One of the features of Martin's oddness was a tendency for obsessive perseverance when a topic caught his interest. At the time of referral, the parents had proudly reported his knowledge about the Beaufort Wind Scale. Martin used this to make endless obsessive calculations about distances between places. Later on, he developed a passion for acquiring facts about the planets. His therapist, noting the repetitive, non-related aspect of his interests, viewed them with some dismay, particularly when they took on a repetitive, auto-erotic quality. The parents, however, in a rather poignant search for an area in which they could invest in their son, related with pride how they gave him complicated sums to do. It was more as a result of the therapist's bland alck of interest rather than anything verbalized that they finally understood that this was a symptom that alarmed rather than pleased the therapist and was not to be encouraged. In contrast, she expressed delight and relief when

Martin finally gave up reading encyclopaedias and became engrossed in more imaginative fiction.

Mrs F had great difficulties in understanding her son's communications, which were admittedly obscure at times. Comments he made appeared objectively disconnected to her, whereas they had an affective sense for Martin. For example, they had gone for a walk, but it had been cut short because it had started to rain. Martin did not respond to his mother's denial of his disappointment, with her jolly comments about the surroundings. Suddenly he announced: "We have 24 meat knives, 24 meat forks, 24 fish forks but only 23 fish knives." His mother felt despair at what she felt was her son's madness and rejection of her attempts to make things cheerier. The explanation for his cryptic utterance was that around this time Martin, unasked, had delighted and surprised his mother by laying the table for a large party. He was proud of his achievement and was praised by his parents. It was possible to empathize with the mother's irritation and frustration and also to explore with her how Martin's inability to express his distress at the failed outing had caused him to recall and repeat an event that had given mutual satisfaction. At first, the mother was defensive, saying disdainfully (as she often did), "Well I'm not a therapist". At the same time she was able to comment fleetingly, "Poor lamb", recognizing Martin's struggle and thus not simply regarding him as a consciously provocative and mad child.

Much of the work would centre on making or uncovering such links between behaviour/events and underlying feelings so that Martin's inner states could be more transparent to the mother. In poignant moments, Mrs F could show her pleasure in having understood her son's underlying feeling state, and the sheer relief at having made a connection could transcend her defensive abrasiveness.

It is admittedly a very delicate and tricky situation when the therapist holds an understanding that the parent is working towards. This therapist at times felt desperate in working with the parents, but she felt equally desperate at times when working with their son and so was able to appreciate their helplessness and exasperation. She constantly acknowledged that the analytic setting provided a shelter where divergent stimuli were reduced to a minimum and gave Martin a framework that even the most caring parents would find difficult to cope with in a family situation.

When the father thought about his child and the analytic gains he had made, he was fearful that the improvement would not hold. The mother, on the other hand, welcomed the gains as an indication there was nothing wrong with her child. The therapist had to carry and contain the despairing aspects of their attitude, but this was tempered by the very real gains he had made. On the other side, she had to maintain a realistic view of his progress and not enter into the mother's unrealistic hopes. Perhaps the most crucial aspect of the therapist's interaction with the parents was her undisguised regard and admiration for Martin's struggle to achieve ego control and age-appropriate behaviour. Her approval and fondness was transmitted to the parents and, in turn, through identification with her they could release their own nascent positive feelings. It was this affective alteration that then allowed them to acknowledge his limitations and free him a bit from the burden of damaging expectations. Perhaps this was an example of parent work enabling the parents to hold their son in their hearts as much as in their minds.

Vignette 3

The third vignette explores a therapist's work with the mother of a child she was concurrently seeing in analysis where there was a strong investment by the parents in the child's remaining as she was. Through her, the parents could deny all conflict within the marriage. Above all, via externalizations and projections, they could avoid any awareness of conflict within themselves. In this case, the mother was not at the point where she could recognize and reflect on her child as she was. She was compelled to use her for her own psychic needs and identified her with feared and hated figures from the past. Clearly, if treatment for their daughter was to have a chance, work with the parents would be crucial, firstly so that they would not withdraw her from treatment, and second, to enable them to see her as she was rather than in the light of their own externalizations. However, the process of disentangling the child in the parents' mind from their own defences, so that she could stand as she was, meant that their whole defensive system would be threatened, so there were risks. Underlying the risks involved in change seems pertinent. After all, when a family refers a child for help, although they are declaring a difficulty, the very difficulty may represent an attempt to make an adaptation. The family members' psychic functioning may be aimed at a homeostatic balance that will keep further terrors at bay.

By the age of 8, "Vera" had been seen at several clinics, but all attempts at intervention had broken down. At the time of referral, her parents, Mr and Mrs G, were afraid that she would hurt her younger brother. Consciously, her life was taken up by her hatred of this brother. Vera could not bear closeness. She was also extremely controlling in her demands and verbally abusive. At school she was friendless but functioned adequately. In the beginning of her analysis, she did not want to come. She presented herself as a hating and hateful child. It took a long time to reach her terror of allowing any loving feelings.

At first, the mother too was reluctant to come, particularly as this implied that Vera was not the sole carrier of all difficulties. The father refused to come. For the mother, there was enormous shame and secrecy about having a child in need of help. The question facing the therapist was how to work with a mother where there was little awareness of psychic processes that would enable them to look at the mother–daughter relationship together. Under what sort of "contract" could the work occur? To begin with, the therapist enlisted the mother's help as an ally and validated her importance as Vera's mother, saying that she, the therapist, would need mother's help to support her work with Vera. The therapist also offered the mother help in understanding Vera's reactions as a way of finding ways to help Vera. It was evident that this "contract" did not involve being mother's therapist but, rather, being someone who could help her be the "good mother" she wanted to be. For the first year, Mrs G came reluctantly and defensively. It was only when her constant expectation that the therapist would find her a bad mother diminished that she could begin to speak about her true feelings towards her daughter. She could then voice her hatred and her sense of duty that dictated that she must continue to mother her. At this point, she began to attend more frequently and would arrive on time.

Against this background of safety, the therapist and mother could begin to think together about some of the fears that lay behind Vera's aggressive behaviour. This work had a twofold result. It enabled mother to begin to see her child as a vulnerable human being with her own feelings, fears, and wishes. At the same time, the therapist's attempts to understand what was going on in Vera's mind in interactions at home served as interpretations in displacement of what might be going on in the mother's mind, at first without this having openly to be clarified at all. The therapist writes:

"It seems to me that this preconscious application of child-centred interpretation to the self is something many parents do. It can enable mothers to tolerate aspects of themselves which in individual therapy can be much harder to reach. That is, I believe that in working with a parent, even though the child is the overt focus of work, we have a unique therapeutic opportunity—although, of course, much working through has to be done outside sessions. Where mothers can tolerate in a child what had been intolerable in themselves, the unbearable becomes bearable."

In this process, the changes in both mother and child are mutually enabling. The therapist quoted above delineates how a parent can work in displacement with the focus on the child. Other parents may be able to tolerate a more direct focus on themselves. The question for the therapist is sensing which will be most fruitful. If, however, the mother is unable to change, then the child may have to obliterate any growing awareness of previously intolerable aspects or to abort progressive developments. Where a mother and child are as closely enmeshed as were Vera and her mother, the same issues are often alive simultaneously in the work with each. They come together naturally in the mind of the analyst. Within the session, the focus is on the particular patient, but outside the sessions there is a preconscious processing that draws on and makes use of the affects arising from the work with both the parent and the child.

For instance, the issue of mother's murderousness was presented by both mother and daughter within the same time frame. The material of each remained confidential. It was only in Vera's second year of treatment, through the transference and the countertransference, that her suicidal wishes were linked with her view of her mother as a murderess. At around this time, Mrs G was able to let go her previous idealization of her own mother and openly admit that she felt that her mother had been too depressed to engage with her.

Over time, the idealization that Mrs G had defensively used to think about all relationships began to crumble, giving place to a range of powerful affects including resentment and jealousy. When she began to talk about her own jealous feelings, she no longer needed to deny Vera's hatred of her brother. Interestingly, it was only after the mother had been able to admit to her own jealousy and guilt that Vera could admit hers. Most strikingly, after this, Vera remembered that her hatred of her younger brother had been exacerbated when she witnessed his jealousy of a cousin who came to live with the family. Thus, she had employed towards her brother the same mechanism of externalization that her mother had employed towards her. Freed from the need to deny her guilt about hating and jealousy meant that she could move into a position where she could cope with having a brother.

The therapist worked with the mother towards recognizing her underlying feelings of hatred and tried to help her to modify or withstand her very harsh superego which felt them to be so terrible. Mrs G was driven by a need to be perfect, and any slight slip was experienced as catastrophic. She became aware of this when a minor slip-up in an otherwise successful holiday she had arranged for her family was experienced as a veritable trauma. She could not but be aware of the inappropriateness of her reaction and the extent to which an inner critic ruled her life, since everyone else had praised the successful holiday. She commented that perhaps in some ways she was like Vera and hoped that what she had gone through would help her to understand her children. This gave her motivation to work on her own difficulties, and work in the third year was more overtly in relation to these. More consistent, interpretative work could also take place. As Mrs G began to recognize her own needs, she and Vera could have moments of genuine closeness; at the same time, she became more honestly resentful about Vera's demands and so could set better limits.

Working with both the parents and the child gives rise to a number of questions, most importantly with regard to the development of the transference. It has been suggested that such work may mean that the child will see the parents and therapist as in alliance and that the transference will tend to reflect only the current relationship to the parents. Certainly, in the beginning, Vera's relationship to her therapist did reflect her general mode of relating to not only her parents but almost all her objects. Later, the positive affects that were released by the analytic work were initially made manifest in relation to her mother, while the therapist continued to carry the negative transference.

It has also been suggested that sessions with the parents interrupt the ongoing work with the child, which is deflected by her concern about the parental sessions. This may be the case where the pathology is less over-determined or kept alive by the ongoing relationship with the parents and is fully internalized. However, with Vera, her preoccupation with maintaining a hating defence left her largely unaware of her objects other than as they directly related to her, and her awareness of work with the mother barely impinged.

Vignette 4

In the final vignette, the therapist worked with parents who, each by virtue of their own pathology, had an enormous and ultimately developmentally distorting, narcissistic investment in their child. The therapist found working with the father, in particular, challenging.

"Tancred" was referred to The Anna Freud Centre at the age of 7 years because of severe learning and behavioural problems. The parents, Mr and Mrs H, had only accepted the referral to avoid exclusion from school. In the assessment process, it became clear that both parents had assumed that their first-born child would be special—a genius. Their entire attitude to their child and their handling of him was predicated on the notion of his uniqueness and specialness, as reflected in their choice of name for him. His precocious development confirmed and strengthened their belief. In brief, they did everything possible to establish and maintain his feeling of omnipotence. In parallel, they believed that they could protect him from all danger and frustration.

Tancred was offered five-times-weekly analysis, and the parents were offered work with an experienced psychiatric social worker. The parents would not cooperate with their worker, demanding to be seen by their child's therapist. Finally, in order to protect the treatment, it was agreed that Tancred's therapist would see them once per fortnight. In a sense, their omnipotence had to be colluded with. However, the therapist in her focused work with them found Mrs H accessible to a more realistic view of her son's disturbance. Mrs H, who was less involved in Tancred's problems than was her husband, began to appreciate how she could help her son. She was willing to gradually introduce more age-appropriate demands on him in parallel to his growing understanding of his real authentic potential, independent of omnipotence. Mr H's own narcissistic needs remained all-pervasive.

The following segment illustrates the difficulties. Tancred had been having nightmares, which Mrs H linked to a recent accident reported on TV. There had been an accident on a big dipper in which a child had been killed while his parents watched. In treatment, Tancred had screamed his terror that neither the powerful parents nor his therapist had been able to save the child. He clearly felt his omnipotence had been punctured through the parental self-object's failure to protect the grandiose self. The therapist verbalized Tancred's distress that the parents had not been able to protect their child. Mr H exploded, leapt to his feet, thumped the table with his fist, shouting, "I can't be God Almighty, I couldn't have saved him". He stormed out of the room, knocking over a chair and, as the therapist subsequently learnt, got drunk and crashed his car.

This last vignette lays bare the difficulties of working with certain parents. Tancred's therapist expressed the view that it was possible to find small windows into self-awareness and some awareness of the child's needs, but if interventions were mistimed, the effect was disastrous; contact was lost and grandiosity of the self reinvested. Therapists working with such parents are confronted with difficult questions about their therapeutic position. One has to work very hard not to become a persecuting object, but this must be counterbalanced by the opposite risk of colluding with their omnipotent defence. Is there a position to be reached where the therapist neither challenges nor colludes in order that the treatment can be maintained?

In other, less difficult cases, one of the dangers in rendering a "finished" clinical account is that retrospectively the work can be given the gloss of ease. Often the reality of the immediacy of the clinical encounter is that the therapist will be operating tentatively. She will be engaged in a continual process of responding and reflecting, picking up on the moment and closely watching to see how interventions are responded to—which of them bear fruit, and which wither.

* * *

The child revealed in a parent's narrative is a complex being, spun in part from contemporary reality and in part from the parents' own internal history and accommodation to themselves. Quite often, by the time parents refer themselves and their children for help, something about the complexity of their feelings and understandings about their child has been eroded. There are, of course, complex reasons why this is so. Perhaps, then, the task is not just about creating a space to think about and respond to the child with the parent, but about ensuring that the space is both large and deep enough to allow for the restoration of the complexity of the child.

CHAPTER THREE

Keeping the child in mind: thoughts on work with parents of children in therapy

Ann Horne

here is, amongst child psychotherapists, great flexibility in the kind of work undertaken with parents. Furman (1991) describes long-term careful work via the parent, enhancing understanding and offering support on an ego level to the mother of a bereaved boy, typical of the skills developed in her setting at the Hannah Perkins Nursery in Cleveland, Ohio. Winnicott, throughout his writings, gives rather bravura demonstrations of consultations to parents with amazing impact (e.g. Winnicott, 1971). The development of parent/infant work around the world has allowed early, brief intervention enhancing the attachment process (e.g. Daws, 1989; Hopkins, 1992; Stern, 1995). It is not the intention in this chapter to cover such multiple and developing applications of psychoanalytic understanding. Rather, the simple process of the child psychotherapist working with the parent or significant carers of children in therapy is addressed.

It is part of the training requirements of child psychotherapists in the United Kingdom that trainees work regularly, under supervision, with the parent(s)/carer of a child who is in therapy with a colleague. This requirement has not arisen inconsequentially. To some it might appear as one response to changes in social work training in the 1980s, which gave rise, on the one hand, to an emphasis on cognitive/behavioural therapies more readily open to research and, on the other, to a preoccupation with child-protection work of a more managerial, coordinating nature—to the detriment of the capacity to undertake psychodynamic parent work. The economics of the time also led to serious difficulties in multi-professional staffing for many child and family mental health settings, psychiatric social workers especially being casualties of cuts in local authority funding.

The need for experience in work with parents, however, is less pragmatic than a response to financial constraints and professional trends. For the child psychotherapist working with the child, and focusing particularly on the internal world and the sense the child has come to make of himself, it is all too easy to identify solely with the position of the child. There are several influences that lead to this pressure:

1. The polarization of "poor child/awful parents/good team" is one that all child and family mental health services practitioners have to deal with. We often, as child psychotherapists, work in teams where "causation", "diagnosis", "treatment", and "cure" are concepts used daily. The interactive nature of aetiology challenges us to think with subtlety about the complexities of children-in-families, to consider evolving and interdependent influences of nature, environment, growth, family history, myths, and expectations. It can be easier to fall back simplistically on notions of pathogenic families—a view current in psychiatry in the 1940s (see Klauber, 1998) and exposed by Tischler (1971, 1979) in two seminal papers on working with parents of psychotic children. Indeed, it may be that the tone of early writing on object relations theory and child analysis allowed this polarity to be rationalized, as it can seem as if parents are a nuisance factor in analysis (Klein, 1932, p. 76). It is essential, therefore, that there is a shared awareness in clinic teams of the transference *and countertransference* processes at work when we engage with emotionally distressed children and young people and their families.

2. For many parents, the sense of shame with which they come to our services acts as a powerful reinforcer of the sense of "bad" or "imperfect" parent—a projection onto the team of the parental sense of failure with the child, and one that must be addressed in parental work. This can be expressed in a number of ways, many of which might seem antithetic towards a therapeutic relationship: the avoiding parent, the enraged parent, the criticized parent. Indeed, if one considers the process of the primitive defence of projection, it is understandable that those feelings projected are expected to be returned in full force by the object onto whom they are projected—one good reason why parents may find attendance at a clinic difficult. The role of the parent/worker, therefore, must give space for a process of containment that allows the processing of primitive feelings and feeding then back in a digestible way (Bion, 1962a). It requires careful engagement and exploration to determine whether a "good-enough" working partnership can be established with the parent to enable therapy for the child to be a treatment of choice.

3. Working with parents, for the child psychotherapist, also involves the capacity to think and understand the processes that occur in systems around distressed and disturbed children. As Kolvin and Trowell (1996) note in relation to sexually abused children, there is a tendency for professionals in networks to mirror the positions of individual family members. To this can be added the reenactment of family defences and processes, as well as of the internal world of the child (Horne, 1999). It is important, therefore, for the trainee child psychotherapist to have an experienced supervisor who not only is aware of the internal world of the individual parent, but can hold a position where thinking about the polarities and projections in the family system and in the network is possible.

4. Finally, there arise challenges to our concepts of what is "good-enough" parenting (Winnicott, 1965). The omnipotence of the clinic team may intervene; the need to assess risk where there *are* serious concerns about parenting; one's own experience of childhood and sense of shortcoming; or a theoretical base that does view the dyadic relationship as "causative" of childhood

psychopathology, not allowing the parent the same sense of an interactive experience which pushes him or her to adopt a position in relation to the child, just as the child's experience leads to the position he or she adopts—all these meld together. It may be simpler to opt for a "bad parent" position in the face of the complexity of the reality!

The nature of parent work

There has long been a debate around the *nature* of "work with parents" as undertaken by child psychotherapists: is this psychotherapy for the parent? Does it support parenting? Or is there a complex and quite sophisticated route to be taken whereby psychoanalytic insight and technique is applied to the unique experience of being a parent of a child in difficulties? The Association of Child Psychotherapists is clear about the first of these propositions:

> Students must have experience of working with parents: either those whose children are in treatment or those where the work is focused on the child or adolescent. This is not adult psychotherapy. [ACP, 1998, p. 5]

It has been suggested that one can move into psychotherapy for the parent if given permission by the parent. This author finds that to be uncertain ground, although the ACP merely comments that, if a trainee child psychotherapist is engaged in adult psychotherapy with a disturbed parent, a different experience of working with parents remains necessary to complete the training requirements (ACP, 1998, p. 5).

The contract with the parent is normally one concerning the treatment of the child. The focus of work, therefore, although it may well clarify those parental concerns that inhibit the development of the child, should be child-focused. If the needs of the parent become open to analysis, it makes sense to refer to adult colleagues, to allow the parent confidentiality and privacy on personal issues, while continuing contact in relation to the child patient. This may seem unnecessary to those qualified as both adult and child psychotherapists; for the child, however, it retains the sense of the centrality of the child service while taking seriously issues that belong to the parent and are therefore separate from those of the child.

Example

"Megan" was referred, aged 8 years, by her primary school, which was concerned about her inability to concentrate, her inappropriate and indiscriminate affectionate overtures towards adults, her lack of friends, and her seemingness to set herself up for teasing. The head was afraid of her mother, Mrs J, who was prone to violent outbursts when called to school and who seemed hostile to Megan. Megan had been subject to a series of hospital investigations for stomach complaints, missing much time from school.

Mrs J and her new husband (Megan's stepfather, a likeable but ineffective man) attended together to discuss their perceptions of and difficulties with Megan. It emerged over several weeks that, for Mrs J, the presence of a daughter was a vivid ongoing reminder of her own abusive childhood and violent first marriage, in which Megan had been conceived by rape. When veiled hints of Mrs J's violent feelings towards Megan began to appear, Megan in her therapy began to talk of her sense that her mother hated her and wished her dead. Mrs J was perturbed by her own degree of disturbance, and it became clear that Mr J found this terrifying and could not be a guarantor of Megan's safety. Work in partnership with the parents allowed an approach both to social services and to adult mental health services, and a professionals' meeting enabled a "shared care" plan to be developed. With Megan safe, Mrs J was able to talk to her psychiatrist about her compulsion to kill Megan—for example, her need to take back-routes from the supermarket in order not to enact a fantasy of pushing her under a bus.

Once Mrs J had moved to adult services, contact was retained via the therapist who had first worked with the parents. It became a further part of this therapist's role to help the adult service to keep the child in mind: when Mrs J dropped out of treatment and the response of her team was that "character disorders are impossible to treat", it was vital to engage the adult team in risk assessment and strategies for containing the anxieties of Mrs J, Megan, Mr J, and those responsible for Megan. Megan continued her psychotherapy for several years before she moved from foster care (with supervised access visits) to a residential school and worked hard on issues of parentability and responsibility for her mother's psychiatric problems. She writes to her therapist still.

When the child psychotherapist working with the child sees the parent

In some instances, the child psychotherapist will meet personally with the parents of the child, without the need to engage another team member in the process. This tends to occur most frequently and easily in work with under-5s, where there is an expectation on the part of the child that all adults in his orbit retain a total knowledge of him and his feelings—an omnipotence that can enable the parent–therapist relationship to flourish. It is, however, also possible in work with latency children where symptoms are of a more neurotic nature and where the parents are able to engage with the therapist in a working partnership requiring less parental support. Issues of confidentiality remain important when setting up such a strategy, however, and need consideration first. Such work will traditionally be limited, often involving termly meetings where progress and concerns can be shared. The purpose, as Rustin writes, is

> to sustain a co-operative relationship between therapist and parents, to give the therapist a sense of the child's development in the family, at school and in the wider social world, and the parents an opportunity to enquire about the therapy and test out their confidence in the therapist's capacity to help their child. [Rustin, 1999, p. 87]

This approach to engagement with the parent(s) probably developed from the initial style, taken from the total confidentiality of adult psychoanalysis and applied to child analysis, of meeting with the parent at the start of therapy and then having only minimal contact, preserving the purity of the transference, and keeping the therapy and the child's wider environment separate. It takes quite an integrated, "grounded" parent to be able to cope with this, and as a technique it must often have felt both condemning and excluding of parents. Review meetings will offer sufficient parent contact when the therapy is established with good-enough trust between parent and therapist, and where there are not issues in being a parent that intrude into the progress of therapy, denoting that regular parent work is indicated. They can also be a useful adjunct to regular parent work by a colleague, where child psychotherapist, parent(s), child, and the colleague meet for review, with the child's agreement.

It can happen that the child's therapist is the only worker engaged with the family, although this may well be a rarity. In such situations, there are obviously dangers of a split transference—equally important to keep in mind when there is a "reviewing" role to fulfil. Perhaps we have become more accustomed to this and to handling it. It is now commonplace to anticipate the child's transference to the entire clinic, for instance, often including receptionists and cleaners as well as the waiting-room and therapy-room, and to accommodate and integrate this in the work. It can, however, leave one vulnerable when one engages with the wider network.

Example

"Sally"'s therapist was asked to attend a review meeting, in school, by the school and by Sally's father, a widower with five children. Sally had been in three-times-weekly therapy for eighteen months. This was proceeding well. Her father met monthly with Sally's therapist. The family therapist who had engaged in time-limited work with the family had both completed this and left the clinic.

From being a withdrawn, sad child who could not learn, Sally had begun with delight to learn and to engage with others. Her overenthusiasm and liveliness, however, verged on rudeness at times as she lacked the social skills to manage her new-found "self". Her father, a polite man, upset at this report from school and only hearing criticism, turned to the therapist: "But she is not rude with you, now, is she?" Sally was actually now quite challenging in therapy. The therapist felt very trapped and offered rather lamely that Sally was not rude as therapy wasn't quite about that.

At her next session, Sally bounced in, gleefully stating, "You told porkies in the school meeting!" ["Porky-pies" = "lies" in cockney rhyming slang.] As the therapist struggled to formulate her answer, Sally said, "It's all right. I *know* it's different here!"

Perhaps children sometimes cope better with the problems of split transference than we manage to do ourselves.

A less usual but extremely creative use of the model of the child psychotherapist working with the parent as well as with the child is described by Iris Gibbs (1998) in her paper on non-intensive psychotherapy with 6-year-old "Emma". Following a failed adoption, Emma came into treatment with Mrs Gibbs and, 30 months later, was successfully adopted:

> The first 6 months in the adoptive home was very difficult. Emma pushed her mother to the absolute limit. She began to have dreams that she was handed back to Social Services. Emma refused to let her mother do personal things like comb her hair. She would come from school to her sessions with holes in her new tights and in her new clothes. She kept falling off her bike and was covered in bruises. In the sessions Emma deliberately played up to me and was often cruel and denigrative to the mother. Yet she insisted that mother came in for part of the session. Gradually the situation began to shift. I watched Emma's painful attempts to get close to mother by playing with her hair, by touching, sniffing, licking her. This was difficult for mother but I was impressed with her capacity to tolerate this. In this respect, Emma was like a baby discovering the smells and sounds of mother for the first time. In another way, she was taking a chance on showing the imperfect, damaged, unworthy bits of herself. [p. 10]

The creativity, instituted by the child, in engaging the therapist in work involving the parent in developing a parenting relationship was met by the flexibility of the therapist, rather as Winnicott (1965) describes the primary creativity of the infant being met and encouraged by the mother. It is, perhaps, important in all our work that we do not impose artificial boundaries regarding what is therapy and what is parent-work, but retain the capacity to be responsive in just such creative ways.

When one sees the parent(s)/carers
on behalf of a colleague

Preparation for therapy

> . . . the pregnant woman has to play the role of mother to her own child while still remaining the child of her own mother. The early childhood identifications with her own mother are reawakened and measured against the reality of her relationship to her own child. [Pines, 1993, p. 62]

In this straightforward statement, Pines encapsulates some of the nature of work with parents—a fine balance between holding the child in mind with the parents and helping them separate their own childhood experience (and hence family scripts and expectations) from the needs and actuality of the child. Indeed, some of the most helpful textbooks in this area have been those historically designed for psychiatric and medical social workers and probation officers learning about psychodynamic casework (e.g. Salzberger-Wittenberg, 1970). It may be that, at first referral, it does not seem possible to anticipate parental support of therapy for the child. Indeed, there may be circumstances that contraindicate such a move, however much the clinic team feels that the child could benefit from therapy. There is space, therefore, in parent work, for engagement in preparation for therapy.

Example

Mr and Mrs K were distraught at their elder son's oppositional behaviour, aggression towards his younger brother, and exclusion from school for a violent attack on another boy. "Ali" was 14, the older of the two sons of Turkish Cypriot parents and the carrier of many family expectations. His father thought that hitting him would be effective—but Ali was getting too big to hit; his mother thought his father was to blame by being absent from the family. Ali, it emerged, had taken to sleeping on his mattress outside his parents' bedroom, but no one could explain why.

At the initial family session, the differences between the parents became clearly apparent as they disputed whether Ali did, in fact, need help. Although the clinic team thought that Ali could (and indeed later did) use weekly psychotherapy, at that point it felt as if he were an ambivalent player in the drama of his parents' marriage, drawn oedipally to a role between the parents and without permission to come for help in his own right. It was decided to meet first with Mr and Mrs K to explore their being able to agree on the way forward for Ali and to try to free Ali from his enmeshment in their relationship.

The therapist met weekly with both parents for several months, interspersed with monthly family meetings. An interesting pattern emerged. Mrs K would arrive in the clinic a few paces ahead of Mr K. She would complain—a general litany of being unwell, of Mr K being unhelpful, of her life being so harsh—from her first encounter with the receptionist, and Mr K would mouth mockingly behind her back. Both would go in to their session with this refrain repeating endlessly. The therapist was aware of extreme irritation, anger, and boredom in the countertransference and finally took advantage of a pause to comment on the couple's commitment to their child—they were, after all, attending despite the hopelessness they both constantly expressed, Mrs K by her words and Mr K in his gestures. This rather shocked them. They looked at each other for the first time, and the therapist noted that they seemed perhaps to expect everyone to be hopeless, as if it were no longer possible to experience change. That must feel dreadful. They agreed—it did. (The therapist contained herself: they had agreed, even if about a negative.) However, instead of developing the theme of Mr K's absence (excused by him as "normal in Cyprus—the men meet together") and Mrs K's nagging ("what else to do to tell him?") compounded by Ali's recalcitrance, which was their norm, Mrs K dived into her handbag, announcing that her sister had visited from Cyprus and she had a present for the therapist. She presented her with a blue stone "to ward off the evil eye". The theme of aggression became accessible, initially via the displacement of the need for the protective stone.

There then emerged over the next few weeks a story of sadness and intergenerational issues. Mrs K had been close to her father in Cyprus—indeed, this father had approved Mr K as her husband. They recalled together the days when he "had hair!" and was lively and present. Mrs K's father had died while she was in London, and, although she went home for the funeral, she felt that the three miscarriages she had then suffered were linked to her having let him down. It was much later that she got in touch with her guilt at her special relationship with her father and her inability to make use of her mother as confidante because of this. Mr K felt excluded by the intensity of his wife's grief and by the miscarriages. The passivity of both parents concealed both aggression and great grief.

Both were then able to see Ali as in a similar special relationship to his mother, and that this served the purpose of continuing to exclude Mr K from his wife. They agreed to marital sessions within the clinic for themselves and gave permission for Ali to have his therapy.

Equally, parental hesitation may conceal a complex scenario of shame and guilt.

Example

"Ben" was 6 years old when he informed his mother, Dr L, that he wanted to be a girl. He insisted that he play with girls' toys (Barbie dolls were his choice of Christmas present) and that he would be a girl when he grew up. He drew pictures of the Spice Girls and commented at length on their clothes and hair. His parents were at a loss to know what to do, finding the position that Ben took up to be rigid and unshifting, and his tolerance of family life with his brother and two sisters became limited as he took offence and appeared to feel thwarted at the least provocation. When upset, he would cry with rage and sob uncontrollably. Relationships with peers were uneasy, and Ben was beginning to lose ground at school.

Ben's parents were reluctant to allow him to engage in therapy—he was, after all, only 6. Although as professional people they could hear that help now could well preclude later difficulties, Ben's mother was reluctant to have him "pathologized", and Ben's father passively agreed. Meetings were therefore held with the parents to explore approaches to Ben's behaviour.

In these meetings, there emerged a history of miscarriage, illness, and risk to mother's health that made Ben's presence seem miraculous. Dr L glossed over her feelings about this child whom she had been advised not to have, following the difficult earlier birth of Ben's sister, and about the husband who had colluded with her pregnancy, seeming thereby to prefer the son to the wife. With the therapist's help, she was able to engage with her fears and the anger she felt at child and husband, and her husband was able to describe his impotence in the face of her greater medical knowledge and his terror that he would lose his wife. Ben emerged as the unwitting receptacle for all the unconscious rage. Ben's mother, in particular, felt that she had made him wish to be a girl by her hatred of him in the womb.

His parents, aware that they had issues to explore about being a couple and that many of these, belonging to the couple relationship, were being avoided and voided through Ben, accepted a referral for marital work that would focus on the adult couple (Ruszczynski, 1993, describes this approach). It then became possible to set up regular therapy for Ben. The parental therapist remained involved, albeit less frequently, with Mr and Dr L, limiting the role to reviewing the therapy and helping the parents with strategies around Ben's wish to cross-dress and be a Spice Girl. That this was undertaken by the parental therapist was deliberate: it protected Ben's therapy and also his therapist from the risk of further projections, while the parents gained insight and confidence from their marital work, and it offered them a worker who had heard their personal concerns yet was still very much available for them and able to address them as concerned parents.

Partnership

For many parents, the key to successful parent work is "partnership". This may force us, as psychotherapists, to rethink some of the positions that we take up in relation to our patients. It is not helpful to the black father, ashamed of his son's delinquency, to say to his proffered hand on first meeting, "I'm sorry, I don't shake hands", however psychoanalytically sound this may be in other contexts. Part of the process of parent work must be an approach that invites the parent/carer into an attitude of curiosity about the child, and about his or her role as parent, and that aims to strengthen the parental function.

It is particularly when the parent comes to us with a sense of shame and failure that engagement with the parent as a partner in the work with and for the child is of benefit.

Example

"Jasmine" was a young, single Afro-Caribbean mother living in a South London housing estate where poverty, delinquency, graffiti, and vandalism were rife. Her older daughter, "Rose", was in difficulties both in school (where she was not learning and was beginning to truant) and at home, where her mother found her oppositional, angry, and disobedient. Jasmine had an all-too-vivid sense of racial stereotypes and acute embarrassment about her difficulties. The therapist found her hard to engage, cancelling appointments and avoiding contact. She offered a home visit, and Jasmine accepted the offer. On her own territory, she was transformed—proud to show how she kept her house and how she was managing on a practical level. This less usual engagement, reinforcing a sense of competence and containing a subtle shift in power that the therapist recognized and enabled, allowed her then to express her sadness at how she could not cope with Rose and her fear that the white worker would see her as yet another inadequate black mother—and the tentative start of a treatment alliance was born.

Within this process of working with parents, one will also be aiming to contain those feelings of envy that may intervene in the progress of the child's therapy—one of the main reasons why it works best if a different therapist meets and "holds" the parents and network. This involves not only the parent's envy of the therapist and the fantasized perfect relationship between "therapist-mother" and child, but also the parent's envy of the child's therapy. It was of major importance to Jasmine that she had her own person to call on, especially as she got in touch with her own sense of not having been parented and when she began to be able to articulate her envy of the help, available to Rose, that she had been unable to have at Rose's age. For the child, it is ultimately freeing to realize that the parent has someone of his or her own to talk to: the process gives permission in a way for the child to *have* therapy.

Ego support—especially in the child's real world

It is a part of this "partnership relationship" that the therapist supports the parent's capacities to deal with and engage with the child's environment—school, social workers, even housing agencies. This can entail joint presence at, for example, school meetings, where the role may well become that of "auxiliary ego" to the parent, helping him or her articulate the parental view and supporting this. In this process, one also helps the school recognize the parent as partner. It is vital with the parent to reinforce and develop ego skills and competencies; it is all too easy to assume the role and as a consequence undermine the parental position and authority. It may also, of course, involve gently challenging the parent at times, and a good alliance is necessary to enable this.

"Good-enough" parenting

When one spends one's training learning about normality and pathology, it can be hard to adopt a position where "good enough" comes into one's assessment of the interactions and development of the relationship between parent and child. The powerful emotional impact of the child's experience and sense of himself in the transference may also bias one away from any sense of a functional parent. Yet daily our work is concerned with compromises, and a sense of what the parent can manage, of what can help improve or reinforce that, and of what is "good enough" is essential. For some parents, however, we have to be able to say what simply is not good enough—as this final section shows.

The environment: parental work and the network

It is vital that the child psychotherapist becomes competent at working in and with a network of professional colleagues. Many children in therapy have a range of other adults involved in their care: social workers, teachers, psychologists, foster-parents, guardians *ad-litem*, fostering social workers, and so on. Given, too, that many of the children whom we see in therapy today have had an experience of serious trauma or perversion in their early lives, the parent- or carer-worker will require to have skills in understanding the processes at work in networks. These not only encompass the tendency to take up the individual positions of the family members (Kolvin & Trowell, 1996) but also involve an understanding of how the professional system can enact the defences, anxieties, and relationships of the perverse family network. The parent- or carer-worker then needs to hold an integrative function as central to her work and be able to articulate the unconscious mechanisms operating in the network.

Example

"Angie", age 8 years, was in four-times-weekly analysis. Her father had been imprisoned for sexually abusing teenage girls, whom he also filmed for paedophile friends. His abuse of his daughter emerged on the films and in photographs: she had never disclosed it. Angie's mother received a three-year probation order for her part in the offences. Once in foster care and in therapy, Angie began to recall and talk about the abuse of herself, which had begun when she was a preverbal infant.

The therapist working with the foster carers found an incapacity in the network to plan with any consistency for Angie's future. The child stayed in a short-stay foster placement for two years, despite the foster-mother's reminders to the social workers. An ultimatum by the foster-mother was met by sudden, unplanned change, followed by a further (third) short-term placement. Professionals' meetings were planned with difficulty, then cancelled. Angie's social worker became ill. Angie's mother requested increased access, and an independent expert agreed.

For the therapist, the first step was to *think* about what was happening, in the face of a network that was plainly acting and not thinking. The moves of carer could be seen as a repetition of the abusive early experience, with the child a silent victim but also with the therapeutic team made to feel victimized, impotent, and excluded from decisions. Senior managers in the social services team felt great sympathy for Angie's mother—who had, after all, been married to a horrible paedophile—and lost the capacity to see the mother who had colluded with the abuse of her daughter and the daughters of other parents. It was vital, therefore, to regain a whole, rounded picture. This was achieved by calling in an expert on mothers who abuse, who could challenge the partial perspective that informed social work decision-making. At the same time, the therapist worked with the carers to ensure their understanding of the child and that they felt able to undertake her long-term care. Finally, the evidence already held by the clinic team—that Angie was disturbed by her family contacts and enraged with her unprotecting mother—could be heard and a meaningful plan generated.

The therapist's role in such a scenario not only works to protect the child's therapy, but begins from an understanding of the child's position and struggles to keep the child in the minds of those seduced by the needs of the organization or the abusive parent. As the abusive family denies the reality (or humanity) of the child, so the network repeats that abusive denial. It is not an easy task engaging with perversion in child work: the capacity to think and to think with the child in mind is critical.

Conclusion

There are parallels between work with the child and work with the parent: the building of a treatment alliance; the acceptance of projections and thinking about when and how to modulate and feed those back; ego support. Much of this, however, in parental work takes place at a conscious or preconscious level, working with the functioning ego rather than the unconscious. Indeed, it may be that one indicator of the need for separate work for the parent as an individual, rather than as parent, arises when the material emerging seems to originate more from the unconscious mind.

An experience of working with parents—and, more widely, with families and networks—is essential for the trainee child psychotherapist. It balances the partisan alliance with the child's experience, adds a sense of compromise and what is "good enough" to the certainties one can sometimes gain from theory, and enables a more rounded view of "child-in-family" that can only stand one in good stead for one's future career. Just as one would hope that the child may, through therapy, be able to resume an appropriate developmental path, so parent and child may together find or rediscover the developmental pathway of parenting and being parented.

CHAPTER FOUR

Parental therapy—
in theory and practice

Marianne Engelse Frick

The theme of this monograph—working with parents of children and adolescents who are in psychoanalytic psychotherapy—describes a form of treatment that has developed together with the ongoing specialization of individual child psychotherapy. When we choose this parallel form of parental treatment, our task is defined by the structure of the latter. The term "parental therapy" encompasses many types of treatment, which may appear in very different forms. However, the task field is always the same: to improve the situation of the child, we should not only ensure the prerequisites of child psychotherapy, but also help parents to start or restart a positive parenting process in order to accept and support the results of child psychotherapy.

In this chapter, I concentrate on therapeutic aspects of parental treatment, as described below under "Psychotherapeutic Interventions within Parental Treatment" and "Individual Psychotherapy with the Parents", aiming to help parents to start or restart a positive parenting process. This requires the parental therapist to know typical elements in this sort of psychotherapeutic intervention—that is, to be conscious of the therapeutic role to be performed, the tools to use, and the problems to expect. I illustrate this with some case examples. First, however, I present a survey of the different areas and levels in parental therapy which may become actualized in this type of treatment before the therapist may concentrate on the inner problems of the parents (for a comprehensive overview of the different aspects of parental therapy, see, for example, Armbruster, Dobuler, Fischer, & Grigsby, 1996).

Prerequisites for child psychotherapy and parental therapy

When child psychotherapy seems to be the appropriate form of treatment, the professional team tries to engage the parents in the therapy. The first, obvious motive for the parents to join in the therapeutic process is their wish to help their child to recover. As in all other therapeutic processes, we must at first concentrate on establishing a working alliance. To that end, it may be of use if the parental therapist helps the parents to understand, at least on a superficial level, the problems of the child by describing them in a comprehensible way, perhaps with the help of the results of the psychological assessment.

When we meet parents in this context, we try to set the psychological problems of the child in a psychosocial context. As members in a family, both parents and child are living in a more or less nourishing, vulnerable, and constantly changing system. The parents are dependent on each other, and the child is even more dependent upon them. The therapeutic process usually extends over a period of several years. Therefore, the parental therapist has to be prepared to repeatedly change focus during the treatment, adjusting not only to the child's development, but also to the parents' capacity to understand the child's changing psychic needs and their own possibility to provide a stable environment. Thus social, supportive, and therapeutic interventions are all included in this type of treatment.

The different layers in the motivation of the parents to participate in the process of child psychotherapy constitute another complication in parental treatment. Parents want their children to be happy; at the same time, they need to maintain their own defences. This makes them ambivalent in their search for help. We may find similar resistances against inner change in people treated in individual psychotherapy. But, if we regard a child's symptom as being part of the parents' own problems, motivation and resistance have been located in different people and are therefore more difficult to treat.

The demands on the parents
in the beginning of child psychotherapy

Parallel with the diagnosis of the child, we need to assess the capacity and motivation of the parents to join in the demanding process that follows. This assessment influences the contract we will offer them. For the continuation and subsequent results of the therapy, it is essential to keep up the contact with the parents. Where motivation or capacity in the parents is lacking, child psychotherapy should thus not begin.

In one of my cases, the assessment of the child indicated that individual therapy could be very useful. However, we judged the parents not to be capable of engaging in the process, even on a minimum level. Therefore, the child's psychotherapy was delayed. When my colleague continued a sparse contact with the parents, she discovered that their capacity had improved dramatically after their elder daughter left an institution in which she had been treated for many years. We learned that the parents felt that the institution's staff had blamed them for the problems of this daughter. Apparently, it had been too much for these parents to engage, at the same time, in the problems of another of their children.

If parents demonstrate an ambition to help their child, the parental therapist should start by focusing on those aspects in the life of the child which Winnicott (1963) has described in detail. Winnicott discerns an "environmental-mother" and an "object-mother" function, representing different aspects of the mother asked for by the infant in its shifting moods. The infant needs her "environmental-mother" function of care and "holding", in a both physical and psychological sense (Winnicott, 1960). It relates to her "object-mother" function to satisfy its drives, including both its angry attacks and its longing for the breast. Thus, the child relates to different mother-aspects when it is quiet and when it is excited. A process of integration is initiated on the one hand by the occurrence of intensive drive experiences, which "gather the person from the inside", and on the other by the preservation of the child's "going-on-being", under the protection of the mother's "holding" function. Through this process, the child brings together drive-related and ego-related elements. Eventually the child starts to develop its ego functions as a separate person. (I use the terms "mother" and "parent" as equivalent of each other. The father and the relationship of the couple are basic conditions for a child's development. However, in this context, I regard them as aspects of the environmental mother. They are both part of the holding function of the mother, including the entire surroundings, which influence the well-being of the child, and which it experiences as being under the active control of the mother.)

Social work aspects

Winnicott's "environmental-mother" function summarizes the task of the mother to provide for the infant's undisturbed "going-on-being". An extension of this task may include the total social situation of the family. Winnicott speaks of the "facilitating environment" in this context. Ornstein (1976), who stresses the importance of this element for the therapeutic situation, discusses the need to create a therapeutic environment for the child when starting psychotherapy. Thus, in addition to the ability of the mother to ensure safe care, we can regard the available home situation (e.g. economy, health, and the marriage relation) as part of this therapeutic environment. The parental therapist therefore also needs to check the situation at school, in the day-care centre, and so on. If necessary, the parental therapist may, jointly with the parents, improve the cooperation of those engaged in the care of the child. The parental therapist's empathy for the parents while working with these aspects makes it possible to enhance the holding function of the parents and for them to increase their self-esteem in their parental role.

Pedagogical advice

Another important aspect is that parents who lack positive models themselves may need help to understand how to meet their child pedagogically. Winnicott's definition of the "object-mother" function demands that the mother interacts with the child in a direct and spontaneous way, combined with her understanding of the needs of the child in different developmental phases. The symptoms of the child may demonstrate his difficulties in his learning of giving and taking and in subsequent developmental tasks in relation to the mother. The parental therapist may try to help the parents to handle both the satisfying and the frustrating elements in the education in a more balanced way. This will, in its turn, stimulate the separation–individuation process.

The main focus in this aspect of the treatment is on conscious material. As Ornstein (1976) suggests, the parental therapist, as mediator, has to present the symptoms of the child to the parents in order for them better to understand the child, which will enable them to respond in a more empathic way. In this context, van der Pas (1996) stresses the importance for the parental therapist to ally herself with the parents. They should feel understood in how they experience the child's behaviour.

*Psychotherapeutic interventions
within parental therapy*

If the parents—in spite of improvements in the surroundings of the child and increased knowledge about the child's psychic needs—continue to behave in a destructive way towards the child, the parental therapist needs to consider possible unconscious resistances. It may become necessary to help the parents to process such inner hindrances and resistances for them to meet the child more constructively. Benedek (1959) states that disturbances in parental identifications—due to deficits and trauma in their own childhood, or in their present relation to the child—may cause people to fail in their parental task. The feelings of shame and guilt, which are natural reactions to such failures, may complicate the treatment of the parent and create typical transference reactions (see further below).

Individual psychotherapy with the parents

As a final aspect of parental treatment, it may sometimes be necessary to offer individual psychotherapy to very disturbed parents. Parents can "use" their problems with the child as an excuse to seek help for their own sake. In such cases, the therapist must assess the most appropriate response to the parents. For this, we can use Simcox-Reiner and Kaufman's (1959) description of different phases of the psychotherapeutic process with parents who have character disorders. Also, Carlberg (1985) discusses the often difficult countertransference reactions in psychotherapy with parents of psychotic children, due to the deep regressive dynamics activated by the problems of the child.

Parenthood activates two different types of identification in the adult

When we, together with the parents, have (as far as possible) improved the environmental situation of the child and also clarified some of the child's needs to them, we may hopefully concentrate on the therapeutic aspects of parental treatment. However, my experience is that the parents' motivation to seek help for their child does not necessarily make them willing to deal with their own deficits and resistances. But when the total conditions are "good enough", the parents may become our active partners in the therapeutic treatment of their child, by using the contact with the parental therapist to process their own problems that block their parental ability. When such an opportunity presents itself, the parental therapist should know the psychodynamic processes that are active in the parent–child relationship.

To do so, we, as parental therapists, have to understand which needs the parents have to satisfy in the child (as was discussed above, with the help of Winnicott). If we want to help parents adequately to respond to those needs, we have to look into the corresponding processes activated in adults when they execute their parental task.

Benedek (1959) is one of the major sources for such an understanding. Though her typology of drives (now usually referred to as "affects") has been the object of further development (e.g. by Stern, 1995), it still gives us important insights into these processes, for the purpose of parental therapy. She approaches parenthood as a developmental phase in itself, by ascribing to it its own libidinal impact. In the processes activated in becoming a parent, old traumas and deficits influence how the parental role is executed. Of course, the varying relational chemistry between parent and child also influences the quality of parenthood. Even biological factors in the child, as well as the psychosocial situation into which the child is born, may influence the development of bad or good circles (Winnicott, 1955) in the mother–infant relationship, which Stern (1995, p. 188) describes as the capacity of the mother to create "positive distortions" regarding her baby. By being a good mother, the mother can come to an intrapsychic reconciliation with her own mother. In this way, motherhood facilitates the psychosexual development towards completion in the adult woman.

In her analysis of this process, Benedek discerns two types of identifications that emerge in the woman giving birth to a child:

1. The first is linked to the primary reproductive drive, as an adult tendency to give and nurse. In giving and caring, the mother identifies herself with her own mother. This is stimulated by physiological changes during pregnancy, and, after birth, lactation makes the child the evident object for the mother's drive to nurse. A good mother offers her infant a possibility to introject her as a good mother-object. This creates confidence and self-esteem in both mother and child.

2. The second identification is defined as temporary and more complex. It may be described as a secondary organization, derived from the oral phase of development. Benedek states that each phase of motherhood—like pregnancy, lactation, and even the menstruation cycle—is accompanied by a regression to the oral phase of development. Such a partial regression helps the mother to identify herself with the receptive needs and tendencies of her child.

During the infant's first developmental phase, the more the mother understands and can satisfy its needs, the better. For example, the infant should evoke the mother's own memory of hunger and becoming satisfied. In this regression of the mother, other mechanisms become activated, like the tendency to incorporate the love object. This can be demonstrated by the mother's wish to possess and overprotect the baby. In its totality, I choose to call this the regressive identification of the mother.

However, in its dominating appeal to the mother's empathic ability, this second type of identification must be temporary—that is, reversible. The mother's own experiences also have to enable her to recognize how much frustration is reasonable for the child. Gradually, she has to loosen her identification. In this way, she shifts from magical (empathic) satisfaction of the child to a willingness to read the infant's own signals. From this point on, a development of two separate individuals appears.

Benedek also delineates a corresponding shift in processes of identification in the father. I would like to stress one main difference that she makes between the two partners: regression in the woman is stronger than in the man. This is partly explained by the physiological changes during pregnancy. We should not forget that, for the woman, several parts of her body can only be activated by birthgiving. Such activation creates new libidinal sensations. The woman's act of birthgiving, and the subsequent libidinal activations, are equivalent to the wish of the man to survive in his offspring by genetic contribution (Benedek, 1959; Chaffin & Winston, 1991). According to them, while the woman's main role is to answer to the child's immediate needs, the father's is to provide for his family. For both parents, their adjustment to the state of the infant should enable them to concentrate on the infant with all their love and thereby start the necessary bonding process.

To summarize Benedek's analysis, we can say that the woman who recently has become a mother identifies both with the mothering side of her own mother and with the dependent side of her infant. Her own way of relating to the infant has therefore very much in common with the feelings she held towards her mother. The child does not yet have the same capacity for identification, but it starts to develop its own identifications, with the help of those that the mother and the father are offering.

Benedek's two identifications are both active during all phases of parenthood. What should vary is the gradual shift in emphasis from one to the other. When the child becomes older, problems may emerge as a result of complications in those two identifications. These problems may interact with the present developmental needs of the child. Like Benedek, Offerman-Zuckerberg (1992) studies the parenting process as such. She completes Benedek's theories by presenting a structure of parenting. This structure can help us to disentangle different components in the individual case of parental therapy. Offerman-Zuckerberg discerns the following five phases in parenting:

I. *The transformation of unconscious wish into reality*

—the passive wish for children becomes active reality.

II. *The experience of bonding, attachment, and separation*

—this appeals to the ongoing wish in the adult to be reunited in a symbiotic harmony with her or his own mother. It can be regarded as the foundation of love: "the primordial transference". As parents, a good deal of our understanding of our children is based on mutual projective identification. This is an unconscious process—that is, what we see in the children is partly based on what we ourselves need, wish, and want.

III. *The learning of empathy*

—Offerman-Zuckerberg (1992) sees this as a consequence of the previous phases: "From mental wish to powerful attachment, through separation and psychic loss, comes the learning of empathy . . ." (p. 211) and "The very foundations of empathy reside in the parenting experience" (p. 212).

IV. *The struggle to love and the negotiation of firm and flexible boundaries*

—by providing sufficient attachment, accurate empathy, predictability, and constancy, we make it possible for love to continue.

V. *The change in our understanding of ourselves*

—our children become unconscious targets of projection, symbolization, condensation, and displacement. We engage them in mutual projective identification and we attempt to disengage ourselves from them, to see them more clearly, to interact more responsively, accurately, and empathically with them, and to be in objective time. As we accuse our parents, we assail ourselves, and as we forgive them, we enter into a new existential contract with our own children.

Difficulties in parents as obstacles to child psychotherapy

Benedek and Offerman-Zuckerberg both describe central aspects of healthy parenting. In our clinical work as parental therapists, however, we are confronted with disturbances in these processes.

Defences in parents against their own frustrations, deficits, and trauma

Deviations in the two identification processes described by Benedek can cause many types of disorders. The mother may fail to identify properly with her own mother or with the child. If the identification with the child becomes inflexible, this may be due to unacceptable aggressive impulses, which are reactivated from the oral phase and thereby still alive from the mother's own childhood. Splitting may then be the result, and only dependent feelings may become acceptable. However, the development may also be reversed. The mother does not dare identify with the dependent and needy child, as a defence against her own overwhelming feelings of frustration and aggressiveness, which otherwise would come to the fore. Instead, she may choose a rigid parental identification without empathy.

Deficits and trauma in the mother–infant relationship may make it difficult to integrate contradictory aspects, like love and hate. Splitting—one of the more primitive mechanisms of defence—may be the result of such deficits in adults. Then the subsequent identification processes become impaired or distorted. A dominating use of projective identifications is also a sign indicating problems in the parental function.

I shall not describe all possible pathological developments in the system of defences in people, but only point out some crucial areas in the parenting function, as we meet them when parents seek help. Distortions and impairments in identifications may be seen as a special type of resistance that, together with all the other well-known psychic mechanisms of defence, make up a different and unique pattern for every individual.

As discussed with the help of Benedek, parents need to create a regressive identification with their child at the beginning of the child's life. An inability to gradually slacken this identification may only start to show as the child becomes older. In the relationship with each child, the parents meet in a unique form the projections of their own conflicts. As years pass by, and parents fail adequately to manage their identifications, a split may develop. In such cases, the child's possibility to develop is dramatically impaired, unless the parents receive proper treatment.

Shame and guilt in treatment

Offerman-Zuckerberg (1992) states that "existential guilt that arises in part out of empathy for others is a powerful affect in parenthood". Guilt, in its turn, creates responsibility (van der Pas, 1996), which may be regarded as the motor for fulfilment of parenthood. Shame is an affect of equal importance, theoretically and phenomenologically, to guilt (Block Lewis, 1987; Morrison, 1983), but to which less attention has been paid. Especially when working with parents, we should be able to recognize its dynamics, as well as those concerning guilt.

Shame is the experience of failure of the self in reaching its aims. It produces a feeling of impotence or of being trapped in an involuntary, humiliating situation. This creates aggression or "humiliated fury". Shame and guilt originate in the same experience

(Fenichel, 1946). Guilt may then be defined as a shameful experience, which activates an inner judgement of the behaviour and creates a subsequent need to make amends. When feeling guilt, the person has found a way to handle his or her embarrassing feeling of shame by directing himself or herself towards the person who witnessed or initiated the blaming experience. To ask for a person's forgiveness is a way for the self-esteem to be restored. "It can appear as if shame originates out there, whereas guilt appears to originate within. . . . Both states involve the self in trying to maintain affectional ties to significant others" (Block-Lewis, 1987, pp. 108–109).

Guilt reveals itself in different ways. The feeling can be denied or the affect can become isolated from the situation. It emerges from an inner conflict and is an expression of responsibility. In parents, guilt may motivate them to seek help for their child. However, there is a risk that we as professionals underestimate the intensity of this affect in parents. In the initial contact, it is therefore a delicate task for the parental therapist to handle this feeling, in order not to make the parents feel accused even more. On the other hand, we must not relieve them from this "disturbing" feeling by too much acceptance of their way of being.

When a parent, as a child, has experienced physical or emotional neglect, humiliating treatment, or trauma and never received help to process this, the parent feels shame. Instead of confidence, shame is established in the mother–child relationship, as both confidence and shame originate from the mother's childhood relationship to her own mother. As shame can be regarded as a narcissistic affect, the parent can experience the need to seek help for the child as a narcissistic violation. Block-Lewis accurately points out that the reactions of shame (to hide and to feel trapped) in therapy are often misunderstood as resistances. Thus we incorrectly view such parents as less motivated for treatment. It is, indeed, more difficult to create a therapeutic alliance with them, but this is easily explained by the reactions connected to the feeling of shame and the resulting feelings of low self-esteem.

Guilt is thus experienced as the result of a voluntary act (a moral transgression) that may be forgiven. This feeling is therefore more constructive for the development of the treatment, as it is easier to create a therapeutic alliance with the parents than in cases of shame, in which they want to hide as they feel trapped in the situation. Also, the transference processes tend to become much stronger in cases where feelings of guilt dominate. But when people are feeling shame they perceive others as contributing to the shameful situation by their judging position. To reduce the importance of the other, one may therefore attempt to deny the shameful situation or to deny the significance of the other by not interacting (hiding one's feelings). In treatment, the feeling of guilt may lead to more accusations, which we can deal with, while the feeling of shame may lead to the hiding of important states of affects (as demonstrated in the cases below).

Transference and countertransference

Regular conferences between the therapists involved are a prerequisite for the realization of the parallel treatment of parent and child. Such a coordination may also reduce the risk of splitting, so common in this form of treatment, and help the therapists to use the occasion of projective identification in a professional way. The staff members can help each other not to identify totally with their countertransference feelings and, instead, use them as information about the "state of affairs" in the parallel treatments.

When people seek help for their children, they feel guilty and/ or ashamed. Such states create their special transference and countertransference feelings. As I suggested before, guilt, if not too strong, can be a constructive and motivating factor in the treatment. But there are many other ways of handling this feeling, and the parental therapist should notice this in the transference. For example, the "innocent" parent may be very provoking, enticing us to be accusing or to exaggerate the problems in the child. This may lead to a situation in which the therapists disagree and argue about the diagnosis of the child.

When a parent is ashamed, complications of another type may arise. She or he may hide this feeling and instead become aggressive, without us knowing why, if we miss the shaming experience. When shame dominates in the transference, the therapist easily feels a failure, that she is insufficient. In these cases, the content of the therapy does not explain the resistance, as there are blind spots in the transference. It may take years for the parental therapist to obtain a more complete picture. How the teamwork will develop in such cases depends very much on how the child psychothera- pist reacts to the situation of the child. Is she overidentifying with the child, or is it possible for her to keep some distance from the situation and wait? The risk is that the child psychotherapist expe- riences an acute need for change in the behaviour of the parents and therefore sees the parental therapist as failing if the change is not forthcoming.

Kohrman, Fineberg, Gelman, and Weiss (1971) describe the tendency in child psychotherapists to regress and thereby strongly identify with the child. This can provoke the therapist's untreated feelings towards her own parents. Even parents themselves easily regress because of the trying situation of living with a child they cannot manage. To seek help reinforces this regression because it acknowledges one's failing. The task of the parental therapist is to handle these regressions. It may take time (often more time for parents than for children) to change, which may cause the parental therapist to feel accused by her colleague and/or accuse herself. A parental therapist may also have unprocessed feelings of having had inadequate parents. Instead of forgiving them their failures, she may accuse both them and the parents of the child in therapy!

Because of the regression in children and parents and the great amount of non-verbal material in child psychotherapy, there are always strong feelings in the transference situation. Parents are then inclined to communicate by acting. This inclination is even stronger than in individual therapy with adults in other settings. It may be caused by the tendency of social workers to adjust to others and thereby not to adhere to the outer frame of therapy sessions. Another explanation might be that parents communicate with their children by acting—doing practical things, demonstrat- ing by their behaviour what they mean, but also by their re- gression when seeking help—and thereby bring non-verbal behaviour into the session. Yet another possible cause may be the processes of projective identification. These usually remain very active in severely disturbed families, as Carlberg (1985) pointed out in the cases of psychosis. Projective identifications are also always present in parent–child relationships. They may become reinforced if the parents lack a reflective capacity—that is, the ability to put aside their own needs and consider which answer the child needs. Similarly, the parental therapist may become lost in a stream of unidentified feelings if she does not keep in touch with her reflective capacity.

The role of the parental therapist

Meta-position

Van der Pas (1996) summarizes different frames of reference in defining the task of the parental therapist. She states that his main attitude should be parallel to the parents' own task—that is, to be with the child and at the same time be "above" the child. To simultaneously take and handle these two positions, parents have to use their self-reflecting egos. They have to place themselves in a meta-position from which they reflect on being a parent and thereby find adequate responses to the child's changing demands. Many authors when defining the parental role discuss these two different dimensions. Benedek's two types of identification—with the caring mother and with the needy child—as well as Winnicott's environmental mother and an object mother, have already been described. Analogously, van der Pas describes a "meta" parent and a "work-floor" parent, which also can be discussed as the "reflective" parent and the "participating" parent.

Waksman (1986, cited in Hesselman, 1992) formulates the role of the child analyst: "It is like Hamlet's dilemma: to be or not to be. To be with a child as if you were a child yourself but at the same time to be not a child but an adult who can give the child psychoanalysis" (p. 143).

My own (unpublished) small survey of supervisors of parental treatment corroborates this two-dimensional structure. In psychotherapy, we usually talk of working in depth with the inner problems of the client. However, to explain the experiences of the supervisors I interviewed, we have to add the "horizontal" dimension of working from the outer social problems towards the inner core of the mother–child relationship. To handle the two dimensions of behaviour creates a challenging task for both the parent and the parental therapist, in order to enable the parents to jointly increase their coordinating and integrating functions. It is this challenge that Benedek, Winnicott, van der Pas, and Waksman discuss more theoretically.

The difficulty in jointly handling two dimensions is given a physical analogy in the Swedish labyrinth game. This is a rectangular box with a movable surface and two grips, one on the long side, and one on the short side. To successfully steer a marble through the maze, you have to control the movements of the surface by turning the two grips with coordinated precision. If not, the marble will fall down one of the sixty holes along the route.

Several authors suggest that the meta-function may be compared with the function of the observing ego. This function can therefore not be exclusively claimed by the parental therapist. The stressing of the meta-function of the parent, as well as of the parental therapist, has several reasons. Adults who work directly or indirectly with children are confronted with very open, ongoing differentiating and integrating processes. These processes should be looked upon as a developmental task for the child. The parents should thus guide the child in his growth of a reflective capacity. In addition, when parents are confronted with these very concrete processes in their child, their reactions may reveal weaknesses in their own reflective capacity. In treatment, this may require the intervention of the parental therapist.

Team work

A stable structure of cooperation between the parental therapist and the child psychotherapist helps the parents to remain in treatment. This, in its turn, guarantees the continuation of the child's psychotherapy (Fonagy & Target, 1996). Regular team discussions enable the professionals to help the parents to process their problems as they appear in the parental treatment as well as in the treatment of the child. Hopefully, the parallel therapists may gradually discover that they treat the same themes in their separate but coordinated therapies. When such a parallel process arises, it usually signifies that both parents and child are "working"—that is, that the therapists' attempts to help parents as well as child to process their problems from their respective points of view are successful.

The positive parenting process is therapeutic for the parent

The process of parenting may be compared with the one of psychotherapy. Offerman-Zuckerberg (1992) quotes Freud (1940a [1938], pp. 172–182), who spoke of "after-education" and "the correcting of parental mistakes" in psychoanalysis, and states that much of what a therapist is doing is similar to the task of the parent. The parent allows for a kind of benign symbiosis and facilitates subsequent separation and, after that, the lifelong process of individuation. In this sense, the child psychotherapist is, for a period, taking over part of the parenting. Similarly, the parenting process, if positive, can be defined as therapeutic for the parent. Thus, the special role of the parental therapist should be to help the parents start or restart this positive parenting—the therapeutic process.

Treating inner hindrances and resistances

The parental therapist may have to help with pedagogical advice or counselling of the marital relationship or may have to focus on individual growth for the parent(s). However, these interventions do not reach the core of the problems of being parents. It may be difficult for the therapist to assess the strength of the tendency in parents to isolate or split. There are so many possibilities to escape, so many ways to divert our attention and confuse us. It is also difficult to forecast the development of the child. At the beginning, the child may appear suitable for therapy because of its motivated parents.

When the child develops in his therapy but the parents do not, an impasse in the parent–child relationship probably occurs (Armbruster et al., 1996). If so, the parental therapist will have to help parents to come into contact with their locked-up, unacceptable feelings of aggressiveness, shame, and guilt, which influence their inner representations of the parent–child constellation (as described by Stern, 1995). These representations may become locked in frozen memories and/or fixed feelings, which are very difficult to access in the therapy. It may take years before entrance is given. Defences in parents are often stronger and more rigid than in children, and their changes are more gradual. The parallel treatment therefore often raises special demands on the parental therapist. The often difficult countertransference processes may make the task especially trying. To overcome such obstacles, the parental therapist, besides showing her empathy with the feelings of the parents, should use verbalization, clarification, and confrontation as her main tools but minimize interpretation (Carlberg, 1985).

Illustrations of parental therapy

Thus, when we meet children and their parents in parallel psychotherapy, our task is defined by the combined processes of attachment, of identification and defence, of shame and guilt, and of transference and countertransference. I illustrate this here by a few cases from my work as a social worker, as a child psychotherapist, and as a supervisor of both. This combined background has given me the opportunity to engage in both the process of child psychotherapy and the parallel therapy of parents.

In my work at the child guidance clinics of the County of Stockholm, the practice of child psychotherapy usually allows a frequency of once or twice a week. In most cases referred to in this chapter, at least two therapists were involved. In one case, during my training at the Erica Foundation, I acted as both the child psychotherapist and the parental therapist. This gave me a distinct and intense direct experience of the dynamics between parents and child.

The mother with the violent boy—
a case of frustrated identifications

When his mother worked, a 5-year-old boy (the only child) spent his days at a day-care centre (as do most other children in Sweden). He did not obey his mother or the staff at the centre.

He bit other small children and was therefore transferred to a group for children with special needs. When his behaviour did not improve, the family was referred to our clinic.

In the assessment, done by a colleague of mine, the boy showed strong anxiety and insufficient self-esteem. Both parents were from working-class backgrounds and were not used to therapeutic thinking. However, they were very eager to help their son. They had been divorced for one or two years and wanted to separate their relationship from the problems of the boy. They started a contact with my colleague once every two weeks, while the boy saw his psychotherapist twice a week. After half a year, the mother and father started contacts of their own, with separate parental therapists. The mother wanted a male therapist. After a while, it was hard for this male therapist to continue the contact, because the woman, after at first having been very seductive, now showed a very strong "castrating" aggressiveness. He therefore often felt ashamed when the feelings in the sessions became unbearable.

At that time, the team was unaware of how seriously disturbed this family was and therefore missed the feelings of countertransference of the parental therapist. As a result, the child psychotherapist became very burdened by the problems in the family as well as in the team.

In a discussion of the boy's sleeping habits, his mother revealed that she liked to have intimate physical contact with him. He was often in his mother's bed, even when she was naked. She had developed a cuddling ritual every night when he went to bed. The mother said she could not think of stopping the ritual because she was convinced this would disappoint him, although the boy was 11 by then.

This behaviour revealed that she was caught in what Benedek describes as magical satisfaction. The mother disregarded the boy's signals of aggressive attacks (mostly on others) that demonstrated that he needed an emotional distance.

At the same time, the schoolteacher described the mother's aggressive behaviour towards her son. When the boy disobeyed and shamed her, the mother could say, in a convincing tone, that she would strangle him.

Here the mother demonstrated how her feelings of shame lead to the expression of humiliated fury.

We also learnt that the mother could not bear to hear her son crying as an infant, which made her leave the house. The mother eventually told us something about her own family. Her father, brothers, and sisters all had many serious problems (alcoholism and criminality). Her mother was alive and healthy, but for some reason the mother of the boy did not want to see her.

She thus had great difficulty learning to identify with the caring mother, which she would have needed in order to take care of her own son in a more balanced way. She also tried to escape from the needy-child identification. This she demonstrated by leaving the house when the baby was crying. Later, it was impossible for her to leave her regressive identification, which included her attempts of magical satisfaction of the boy's needs. Instead of growing as a mother, she became filled with agony related to the ongoing development of her child. The mother's fear grew with the increasing physical strength and psychic development of the boy.

Some years after the termination of the therapy with this family, the mother contacted the parental therapist. She wanted to discuss her son's school situation, as he still had difficulties in managing group situations. He became angry very easily and picked fights. When the fighting was brought up again, the parental therapist mentioned his unusual physical strength. Then something very unexpected happened: the mother answered by relating this statement about her son to her fear of her own father, a huge and strong giant, who often had been violent and generally unreliable.

This was exceptional indeed. During all the earlier years of treatment, she had avoided involving herself and her own background in the problems of her child. She had kept as silent as possible about everything connected with her original family, especially about her thoughts and feelings associated with them. Only by this later revelation did we see that her separation of her background from the problems of her child was an expression of her own defences against unresolved problems with her parents.

Now we could better understand her behaviour. Apparently the mother had, as a child, become very frustrated by the threatening behaviour of her father. Fenichel says: "As a rule a frustration provokes an ambivalent reaction toward the frustrating person which may result in an identification with him: the child then becomes either similar or markedly dissimilar to the frustrating person, or to one aspect of this person" (1946, p. 524). As a little girl, the mother had identified with the opposite of her father. However, in this pressed situation as a grown-up she regressed, and her sadistic aggression came to the fore in the contact with the parental therapist. Because of the unresolved identification with her father, she transmitted her expectations of violence onto her boy.

A parent who is fixated in a "frustrated identification" does not make it easy for the child and will obstruct its further development. If possible, this has to be addressed in the parental treatment. As compared to the phases of healthy parenting, we can conclude that this mother was not yet a parent in a psychic sense (cf. Offerman-Zuckerberg's phase III, "The learning of empathy"). If she had reacted positively to our efforts of therapeutic treatment, she could have received psychotherapy for herself. Now, she could never respond to the need of her son for reparation (Klein, 1988).

This illustrates the importance, in demanding cases, of supervision for the parental therapist, the child psychotherapist, and even for the whole team. To better understand such cases, we may benefit from the results of research at The Anna Freud Centre by Fonagy and Target (1996). Their work indicates that the chances for the boy to be cured would have been much better if he and his parents had received more intensive therapy. This would have offered a more containing frame for all the feelings of anguish that "floated" in the family.

The needy daughter and the caring daughter—
a case of splitting because of deficit

Another case demonstrates how the identifications, when intermingled in the general defences system of the parent, may become split up and projected onto two different children.

In a family with two girls, one of the girls started therapy when she was 9 years old. The family was referred to us by the school psychologist because the girl was very uncommunicative and was performing badly at school. The girl was very helpless in her behaviour and appealed to other people's caring. She went to her therapist twice a week, while the parents saw a parental therapist every second week. The girl remained very silent, insecure, and usually rather passive. She had a minor metabolic disturbance, which, however, in itself could not explain her poor functioning. Her sister was her opposite: lively, talkative, with good self-esteem, and good results at school; she also took much responsibility in the family. The parents appeared nice and pleasant. However, it was remarkably difficult to engage the parents in the problems of their daughter. For several years, the mother could not say anything spontaneous about her, while she usually spent a lot of time talking about the other, successful daughter. When we asked the mother about the treated daughter's problems with the teacher and her schoolmates, the mother just laughed and waved it away. Sometimes she could become patronizing. She preferred to stress the girl's physical problems as a cause of the situation.

There was a powerful denial of this girl's problems, especially on the part of the mother. The father, instead, tended to over-identify with the problems of his daughter. It was impossible to help them recognize any problems in the relationship with the girl. When pressed, the mother would even demean the girl and her problems, thus rendering treatment difficult. Because of the parents' attitude, being so nice in the contact with the parental worker, and at the same time being so uninterested in changing their behaviour towards the girl, we can suspect a repression of the parents' experience of deficit in their own childhood.

After several years in therapy, the girl, who remained ill at ease in school, started to play truant. Her sister answered the phone when a teacher rang home to inform the family. A meeting was then organized at school, with the mother, both daughters, the teacher, the school psychologist, and the parental therapist.

This indicates how important the "therapeutic" function of the environment may be. The school staff, who initiated the contact with our clinic, had to remind the parents of the unhappiness of their daughter. When shame is the dominating affect in the treated family, we are usually more reliant on those who meet the child in everyday life to enable the continuation of the therapeutic process. Perhaps it would have served the therapeutic process to have initiated a conference of the school staff, the parents, and the therapists right from the beginning of the treatment.

During this meeting at school, the parental therapist, who had never seen the successful sister before, commented on the beautiful green eyes of both girls. The mother reacted spontaneously by agreeing that their eyes were beautiful, and she confessed that she had always felt envious because of her own "common" grey eyes.

This seemingly trifle statement implied, in reality, tremendous progress. Now, even the problematic daughter was included in the mother's psychic life. In one instant, it cured the split between the different identifications through which the mother's opposite feelings towards the two girls were kept separated.

During the next session, the girl wanted to see her own therapist and the parental therapist jointly. She told them that she had been truant because she thought that her mother did not love her. When the parental therapist confronted the mother with this statement, it led to another positive development in the relationship between the girl in therapy and her mother.

The "niceness" of the parents had made it very difficult for the parental therapist to tell them less nice things. In addition, the feeling of countertransference that caused the parental therapist to be very careful with these parents seemed to be the same as the girl experienced with them. But therapy had made her more daring. In this case of splitting and repression, the only way to address the parents was to be confrontative.

We did not learn any more background details during the mother's own therapy. The little we know is that she bore her mother an ill-feeling and regarded her sister as the privileged one. The mother's family lived in poor circumstances, and from a very young age she had been sent away to contribute to the family's living.

I believe that the mother, and even the father, had lived in such poor circumstances themselves that their feelings of shame were felt as egosyntonic, and therefore the problems with the girl were just "unnoticed".

The lifeless girl—a case of regression because of trauma

In the next case, an acute traumatic experience earlier in his life influenced the father's ability of caring. This event prevented him, as parent, from dissociating himself from the regressive identification with the child.

The family came to see us about their youngest daughter, who was 7 years old. During our introductory meetings, the whole family seemed to be depressed and the girl remained lying on the floor. We were told that she was very compulsive—picking up everything from the street and taking all her dolls with her when leaving home—and so inhibited that she was unable to perform at school. After a psychological assessment of the girl, the staff decided on child psychotherapy. As the case was part of my training as a child psychotherapist, I came to see this girl once a week while at the same time meeting the parents equally often.

Before psychotherapy started, the girl suddenly refused to go to school. Because of this, the outer setting did not function at all when the therapeutic treatment started. The parents had to take turns to stay at home with the girl and to handle the conflict with an insensitive teacher. To handle the school situation therefore became the first topic in the contact with the parents.

After some weeks, the initial crisis diminished, and a working alliance with the parents could be established. In this, a traumatic event in the life of the father was revealed. When he and his younger sister (7 years old at the time) were riding their bikes, she was killed in a traffic accident. Although he was not responsible for this tragedy, he felt tremendous guilt. But the father also felt very aggressive towards his parents, especially his mother, whom he "lost" because of her prolonged mourning. Later in life, it was impossible for this father to set limits for his own daughter. When he took her to an amusement park, he bought her an expensive lunch and had no money left to order himself anything to eat.

The early traumatic event burdened this father with guilt. In being so kind to his daughter, he tried to repair what he had "done" to his sister (making amends). At the same time, he denied his unacceptable angry feelings towards his daughter, whom he unconsciously represented as the sister who had taken his parents away from him. In the transference, the parental therapist felt alternately like a parent who could be appeased, and one who was frightening and big.

The father had presented the death of his 7-year-old sister as a minor fact in his life. Only when the parental therapist actively focused on this event could the father process the guilt and aggression connected with the accident of his sister. He had never spoken about this event before, not even with his own parents. After this therapeutic intervention, the father could set more adequate limits for his own 7-year-old daughter. Now he could accept and support the girl's recovery from her depression and compulsiveness.

The girl without empathy—a case of deficit and trauma

My last case demonstrates the importance of giving attention to traumatic experiences within mother–child relationships.

A family was initially referred to us by the school because of their 8-year-old girl's learning disability and lack of contact with the other children. She was in psychotherapy for four years, while the parental therapist saw the parents once every second week. The parents complained a great deal about the lack of empathy their daughter showed them. The mother illustrated this by describing a situation when she had a headache. Instead of paying attention to the mother's condition by being quiet, the girl, who was 11 years old at the time, started to make a lot of noise while she asked about the headache.

We learned that when she was still a baby, the parents had on several occasions left the daughter with relatives for one or two weeks. And when the child was 1 year old, she had a traumatic experience as she was seriously burnt by a hotplate because of the mother's carelessness. When the parental therapist asked the mother about this incident, the most important fact seemed to be a friend's annoyance about missing the trip they had planned together for that day. Instead of going out, the mother had to obtain acute medical care for her child at the hospital.

Eventually, the mother revealed in the therapy the difficult relationship she still had with her own parents. She saw them as rigid and rigorous people who did not allow much at all and showed little interest in her feelings. Neither were they very interested in their grandchildren, and they could not really accept that the granddaughter had learning difficulties.

Some years later, when the story of the daughter's accident was again raised in the therapy, the mother started crying as she remembered how the girl screamed during the treatment of the burn. It had been very upsetting for her not to be able to do anything herself to relieve the child's pain.

In her first description of what had happened, the mother demonstrated an isolation of her affects of guilt from the actual accident. However, when the parental therapist could offer this mother a thorough acceptance of those difficult feelings, the isolation of the mother's affects of guilt became dissolved. By empathizing with the mother's difficult relation with her parents, the therapist enabled her to come into contact with her own empathy. The mother had felt so guilty and ashamed about the accident that the experience had not been accessible before. But the creation of space to approach her own experiences of having inadequate parents made it possible for her to identify with the needy little child at last. The mother could then become more mothering for her daughter and the girl could show her own capacity for empathy.

Conclusion: parental therapy is often required to sustain the results of child psychotherapy

These and other cases demonstrate that therapeutic work directed towards parenthood, parallel to child psychotherapy, is often a necessary prerequisite for a successful end to the treatment of the child. This is based on the fact that the parental role is an active one, in which the parent has to claim her or his child (Alvarez, 1992). When a child goes into psychotherapy, and the child therapist takes over part of the parenting, this process is out of the control of the parents. The parental therapist is then required to help the parents maintain and develop their parenting responsibility.

To understand the forces active in inner hindrances and resistances, we have to focus primarily on the parent–child constellation. The parental task places a great emotional demand on the couple. By reason of the different types of regression described above, parents are confronted with their developmental shortcomings, in a new and sometimes cruel way (e.g. when they feel they are trapped in situations that they cannot influence).

In several of my parental contacts, despite their active cooperation, the parents came to situations where their own problems prevented them from responding positively to the improved behaviour of their child. The obstacles were mainly their own unresolved traumatic experiences and deficits, either in their own childhood or in relation to the child. These problems facilitated the parent's identification with the divergent behaviour of the child, instead of their accepting and supporting a healthy behaviour. In some cases, the parent's pattern of defences was deeply rooted. To resolve this, the parental therapist had to direct her interventions towards these inner defences in order to develop or to reestablish the original capacity for mature caring.

Together with the need, at the outset, to secure a functioning social setting of the child therapy, this gives a distinctive feature of parental therapy. It has to span a wide range in combining both practical and psychic reality. The diversity of the required therapeutic interventions demonstrates the broad demands on the parental therapists.

In this chapter, I have therefore stressed some of the dynamics and affects that are important in the parenting process. Though they are very central, several elements of this process are not easy to recognize in the throng of all the different themes coming to the fore in the practice of parental treatment. The different realities that we as parental therapists have to deal with—the two identifications activated in birthgiving, the dynamics of guilt and shame, and the special transference and countertransference phenomena connected with all these aspects—make the role of the parental therapists especially demanding. Our meta-function represents the educative task of the parents to help their child to develop its "reflective ego". Hopefully, by studying these processes more thoroughly, the parental therapists will be able to widen this capacity in her or his own professional self.

CHAPTER FIVE

Work with parents of psychotic children within a day-care therapeutic unit setting

Olga Maratos & Athanassios Alexandridis

The focus of this chapter is on work with parents of children with severe psychopathology, diagnosed between 3 and 4 years of age, within an institutional setting. The setting is the PERIVOLAKI ["small garden"] therapeutic unit, which was founded in 1983, initially only for pre-school children; it was eventually developed into a day-care unit for autistic and psychotic children aged 3 to 14 years.

Central to our approach are the following considerations: (1) Autism and early childhood psychoses (symbiotic, confusional, etc.) may have some characteristic features in common, but they also present important differences in mental functioning, affect expression, social responsiveness, and modes of relating to persons and inanimate objects. These differences should be taken into account when working with parents. (2) We are not concerned in our clinical practice with the aetiology of the particular pathology, as the emphasis is put on understanding the mental states, mental functioning, expression of affect, and the ways these children relate to their social environment as well as to physical objects. We believe that the meaning of the child's symptoms should be the primary preoccupation for both the parents and the therapists. Parents' understanding of the ways their children feel and behave is extremely important for the development of their children and for the cooperation needed between the child's therapists and themselves (therapeutic alliance).

The basic theoretical choices and guidelines as well as the organization and rendering of services are briefly presented in the next section so that our approach to childhood psychoses can be better understood and, consequently, the type of work we propose to the parents.

Basic theoretical guidelines

The psychoanalytic approach to early childhood psychoses is considered to be out of fashion, especially among American and British scientists, as many of the discussions during the past decades were focused mainly on the contribution of either organic or psychogenic factors to the aetiology of early infantile autism and childhood psychosis. Kanner's (1943) ambivalent views and Bettelheim's (1967) disputed data and extreme views have made a negative contribution to this debate from the psychoanalytic standpoint. However, for many years the only professionals who accepted children in individual therapy were inspired by psychodynamic theories and concepts such as those of Klein, Lebovici, Mahler, Meltzer, Tustin, Winnicott, and so forth (references to specific points relating to these theories are made in the subsequent sections). These specialists have developed theories about infantile autism and childhood psychosis that were not necessarily related to a search for aetiology. Their theories stress the importance of emotional factors contributing to the psychotic condition and have helped professionals understand better how these children process information and how they relate to other persons and to inner psychic reality.

Rutter (1978, 1983) was among the first to present a cognitive deficit model to explain autism. On the other hand, educational approaches in the 1960s and 1970s were influenced mostly by learning theories based on classical behaviourism (Lovaas, 1977).

As this approach failed to produce any interesting results, it was abandoned, and the cognitive-linguistic approach prevailed over educational approaches offered to these children for quite a long time (Churchill, 1972).

Research into the pathogenesis has been conducted for a long time and is still going on around the world, mainly focusing on the investigation of biological factors contributing to infantile autism and early childhood psychoses. Rimland's (1964) critical appraisal of the psychoanalytic approach was decisive for the beginning of a long era of biological research for investigating especially childhood autism and for separating it from childhood psychosis. The results to date are inconclusive, but researchers are supporting their own theoretical models even when evidence is insufficient. It is our view that this state of affairs reflects the difficulty that we all have in representing the psychotic state of mind, which is confused, fragmented, and overwhelmed by feelings of deep anxiety and panic. It must be stressed that even within the group of those who believe that there is an organic innate deficit in autistic and psychotic children, there are disagreements as to the nature of this deficit: neuro-anatomical systems, neurophysiological dysfunction, neurochemical influences, genetic anomalies are only a few of the factors that are considered to be at the basis of autism. The more integrative present-day theories are grouped in Dawson (1989), and a comprehensive summary of them can also be found in Trevarthen, Aitken, Papoudi, and Robarts (1996).

It is our view that this kind of debate is extremely interesting and useful scientifically but should not necessarily mark the way specialists try to help these children overcome their difficulties. Theories that postulate a basic inability to understand and express emotions seem to open a new way in the investigation of autism and childhood psychoses, as emotion is a fundamental and crucial factor for communication and learning. Trevarthen (1993) has presented an interesting view about the importance and function of emotion in early development. Hobson (1989, 1993) has developed an important theory about autism, emphasizing disturbances in affective development. According to him: "Autistic children have a biologically based impairment of affective-conative relatedness with the environment . . ." (Hobson, 1989, p. 42). These views bring psychoanalytic theories and psychoanalytically oriented therapies of psychoses once again into focus, as, in the work with children, one of the main targets is the management of affect in the way it influences relatedness to others.

The views developed by therapists inspired by psychodynamic theories that put the emphasis on the emotional *deficit* and the affective experience of the child have inspired our own approach at PERIVOLAKI. Kleinian concepts regarding the "schizoid position" and projective identification (Klein, 1946), Meltzer's (Meltzer, Bremner, Hoxter, Weddell, & Wittenberg, 1975) concept of "dismantling", Tustin's (1972, 1981) views on the dichotomy of encapsulation and confusional reactions, Aulagnier's (1975) theory of the "pictogramme" and its importance as the first psychic formation promoting the unification of the self, and Anzieu's (1974) concept of "skin-ego" are, in our view, central for the understanding of mechanisms involved in the mental functioning of the psychotic child.

The theoretical model as well as the techniques used at PERIVOLAKI are inspired by the psychoanalytic theoretical framework, and psychodynamic principles are applied to the organization of services rendered to children, their families, and also to the group dynamics of staff working in the unit. We believe that the psychotic condition that is apparent in the behaviour and mental functioning of each individual child influences not only all professional staff working with the child and his or her family, but also the unit as an institution. For instance, we sometimes notice excessive reactions of professional personnel that often turn out to be a reproduction of the child's or the family's pathology. Frequent and systematic discussions as well as individual or group supervision of the work of the staff help change this type of difficulty in personal reactions to a means of understanding psychotic mechanisms.

The day-care unit and its working model

The unit is a total setting and is the sole point of reference for both the child and his or her parents. Very often it is there that the full and final diagnosis is made and the child is enrolled in a complete half-day special educational programme with a small group of children of similar chronological age; it is there too that the child has individual psychoanalytic psychotherapy and his parents are seen on a regular basis by their own therapists. Most external activities are initially suggested by the staff of the unit, and, by following the family's progress in monitoring the child's activities, the personnel of the unit assist the family either to make only the necessary contacts or to have complete control of all activities external to the unit.

The unit operates independently of a larger institutional establishment, such as a psychiatric or paediatric department of a general hospital—a fact that should be taken into account as this differentiates the relation (expectations, fantasies) that parents and professional staff have towards institutions. Big institutions usually have at their disposal a large number of services available for a larger age span, a fact that creates a feeling of security or even a kind of "insurance" for the child's future. On the other hand, larger institutions also eventually confirm the chronic condition of psychosis and motivate a feeling of imprisonment. A relatively smaller institution like our day-care unit nurtures more personalized relations, a fact that professionals should be aware of as it can be both helpful and dangerous at the same time because of the transference of both positive and negative feelings that are expressed, especially by the parents.

When the unit was founded, it set itself three main aims: (a) to provide specialized services for children with early childhood autism and psychoses and their families; (b) to provide further specialized education and training for child psychiatrists, psychologists, teachers, nursery school teachers, psychotherapists, and social workers who wish to work with childhood psychoses; and (c) to do research into early childhood psychosis, and, more specifically, to investigate the psychotherapeutic process and methodology. The services have been developed and have become more and more specialized throughout the fourteen years of the unit's operation. The fact that the unit receives six to eight trainees from various scientific disciplines and for different purposes (differential diagnosis, teaching, individual child psychotherapy, or parental counselling) every year has been a very positive and rewarding experience, as it perpetually stimulates our way of thinking and helps review our methods of approaching early childhood psychosis. The presence of trainees has also allowed us to organize smaller groups of children with a variety of activities that follow the special interests of the permanent staff, but also quite often those of the trainees—for example, musical-instrument making, puppet making and puppet playing, specialized computer programs, and so on. The third aim is obviously an ongoing one, but it is to be noted that whereas we started following the standard psychoanalytic model and applied it to all the children regardless of age and pathology (50-minute sessions, three times weekly, complete separation of child and family therapy, absolute neutrality of the therapist, and interpretations mostly aimed at transference and unconscious fantasies), we have during the years moved to a more interventive model. The setting remains the same, but some of the children have only two sessions per week and the sessions last only 40 minutes. Furthermore, we have introduced in some of the cases and at specific times during the psychotherapy the use of significant physical objects (blanket, milk or biscuit, potty). Interventions and interpretations take external reality, special events, and the child's secondary process into account, and, most importantly, the child therapist often seeks and has joint sessions with the child and the parents, or with the mother and the child.

Diagnosis

It is to be noted that we believe that there are distinct diagnostic moments as the child develops and that these moments tend to influence the quality of the relationship between the parents and the child but also of the parents' relationship to the therapeutic personnel and the whole setting. At the very early age of 3 or 4 years, when the parents first take their children to specialists, psychosis and autism present many common behavioural features, as the frail defensive system of the young child has few ways of coping with the basic cataclysmic anxiety that is so characteristic of this early pathology. These phenomenologically similar features are withdrawal from social relations, stereotypic movements, and various problems in affective relations and expressive language.

At this very early age, hope for an amelioration is high both among the parents but also among the professionals. This hope is projected through archaic omnipotent mechanisms onto the setting and tends to meet the professional personnel's analogous mechanisms. This obviously influences the quality and content of work with the parents, and it is very important to be constantly aware of any such mechanisms. This is why in PERIVOLAKI there are regular meetings between all the professionals working with each case (teacher, psychotherapist of the child, family therapist, the kinesiotherapist, and periodically the music teacher, etc.) and the case supervisor (child psychiatrist or clinical psychologist). The case supervisor meets with the parents and the child during the first diagnostic period in order to discuss the diagnosis and to explain how the unit works and what is expected from them (in other words, to discuss a form of contract between the unit and the family). The case supervisor then meets separately with the parents at least twice a year and whenever there is a demand by them or by the family therapist.

Children stay at PERIVOLAKI as long as is necessary before they can enrol either at another specialized school more oriented towards the learning of skills or at the normal primary school, usually one or two grades below their chronological age. In both cases, and if the parents ask for it, the special teachers at PERIVOLAKI follow through the child's adaptation to the new educational environment and have regular meetings with the new teachers.

As the child can stay at the unit for a long time (mean stay is three to four years) she or he grows older and the diagnosis is finalized step by step; most importantly, as the chronic condition of the disease becomes more apparent, it is also slowly established in the minds of the parents and of the personnel. The parents are faced with the fact that their child is handicapped and will require their protection and care in the future—maybe even more than at present, with the unit playing the role of a protective "family" both for themselves and for their child. Psychosis—being a devastating condition with a way of mental functioning that has its own characteristics—influences cognitive, language, emotional, and social development; sometimes it also influences motor development, and children can be either extremely dexterous or very clumsy in their gross motor movements. As they grow older, they often give the impression that they are mentally retarded; although in autism mental retardation may coexist with the main dysfunctions of the disease, this is not true for other childhood psychoses. It is actually the psychotic condition that entails various difficulties in cognitive, symbolic, and language mechanisms. The ego of the psychotic child remains immature, and the reality principle malfunctions. The psychotic child's difficulty in representing reality and using symbolic thought in the conventional way that most of his peers do, and in keeping attachments to libidinal objects, influences the way he relates to the external environment and to everyday events. This is the reason why most psychotic children obtain poor scores in IQ tests. These difficulties become more obvious as the child grows older, and the realization by the parents of these specific difficulties is often a crucial moment (positive or negative) in parent–child and parent–professional-personnel relations.

When the hope of a quick amelioration of the child's condition is disappointed, castration fantasies in the parents—and also in the professionals working with the child and the parents—are often revived. These may be followed in the parents by narcissistic trauma, aggression, depression, and later, via working through, to important grief processes. If depression sets in even in one of the parents, this is usually the moment to refer him or her for individual psychotherapy. The work with the parents by the family therapist must follow closely any such changes in the parents' way of thinking and feeling towards their child.*

Work with parents:
setting and psychodynamic principles

Contract

The initial contract made with the parents, in which the types of services provided by the unit to their child and to the family are agreed upon, comprises work by both parents with a family thera-

---

*For more details of the organization of services provided by PERIVOLAKI and the data about the outcome of children's development during the first thirteen years of the unit's life, see Maratos (1997).

pist, regardless of the parents' own requests. It is, in a way, "imposed" upon them. For many years, we followed a strict pattern of weekly sessions for at least the first two years of the child's stay at the unit, and fortnightly sessions thereafter; during that period, we also requested the presence of both parents at the sessions. However, in the last three years we have revised this policy and have been much more flexible in the scheme and the setting of services provided to parents because we felt that it is important to wait for their own demand in order to start any meaningful therapeutic work with them. In the following section, the most recent pattern of work with the parents is described. Work with the parents is undertaken in regular sessions and can occur in the following forms: (a) both parents together; (b) predominantly one parent, with the other one joining in some of the sessions; (c) both parents and the child together; (d) one parent with the child; and (e) brother and/or sister joining in some of the sessions.

Content

The professional working with parents of psychotic children has to face material similar to that produced in any therapeutic work relating to mental functioning: ideas, representations, thoughts, fantasies, feelings, acts with a symbolic character, or acts as attempts at "acting out". This material could be described in terms of the following specific characteristics: (a) a large quantity of extra-linguistic productions, and (b) tension and damage exerted by psychosis on anybody living with it, a condition that influences not only the parents but also those professionals who fail to take the necessary precautions during the sessions. The parents' communications, in spite of the richness and the transference phenomena they carry, cannot be used for the formulation of personal interpretations because we have chosen as a means of therapeutic intervention in our institution cooperation with parents, not family therapy. We believe that the existence of one disturbed member in a family is not by itself a sufficient condition for a family to formulate the kind of deep demand that is necessary for undertaking family therapy. Parents usually need a form of cooperation that might, in some cases, lead eventually to a demand for family therapy. Consequently, interventions by professionals in this setting can only refer to parent–child–institution interactions in any possible form they can take. These interactions should be recognized, explained, and partly interpreted in a psychodynamic way, while at the same time interpretations that refer to the parents' personality structure, to their unconscious patterns, or to imagined scenarios are absolutely avoided. If the professional is able to think of such interpretations, she keeps them to herself and discusses them with her colleagues in the staff meetings described in the previous section. In this way the institution avoids the repetition of traumatic experiences that have been experienced in the family while at the same time acting as a setting where reparation may take place.

Communication

The main and stable concern of the professional during the whole duration of his or her cooperation with parents is the establishment and/or repair of communication between the parents themselves as well as between them and the child, the child and the social environment, the child and the institution, and the parents and the institution. Often, especially at the beginning of this cooperation, communication in these families is quite disturbed and insufficient—if not non-existent. The therapist initially expresses and supports the possibility of cooperation and communication by her attitude: she proposes interviews (i.e. set times for discussions), and she is there at the agreed times for the sessions and available for communication. In this way, she establishes an elementary setting for the parents to attend to. The parents come to these meetings, and through their verbal expressions they initially tend to attack or exclude the other person rather than express their own pain and despair or seek solutions to the problems they are facing. The systematization of the interviews presents the attitude that the parents should adopt towards their child in an exemplary way. The stability in the succession of presence and absence creates the basic condition for the child to begin to perceive the other person ("object", in psychoanalytic language), to establish a stable relation—first in reality and later on mentally.

Cramer and Palacio-Espasa (1993) have stressed the importance of rhythm for normal psychological development, and we have, through our own observations, noticed the absence of rhythm and the anarchic way in which care is provided to psychotic children by their parents. The availability of one specific person with whom parents can engage in discussion symbolizes the continuum "I listen, I understand, I feel, I process the information, I speak" and exemplifies the necessary condition for the establishment of the relation with the maternal object. Bion (1962b) has described this function as the "alpha function". This function is provisionally undertaken by the therapist for the parents of the psychotic child; the therapist processes after accepting and containing within herself all drives for which the other person cannot form representations or relate and recognize as his or her own.

Perhaps this formulation of theory and technique, which is usually related to archaic personality structures, may sound strange and misleading to the reader who might think that we consider or observe psychotic children's parents who have predominantly these types of personality structures. In spite of our observation that within this population there are some individuals with narcissistic personality structures, we do not believe that there is a special psychological profile that characterizes the parents of psychotic children. However, in spite of the variety of personality structures of these parents, we very often observe that, in their reactions and interactions with their psychotic children, they may use archaic mechanisms in what is usually defined as a narcissistic way of relating. The usual condition with which the therapist is faced is a fragile narcissism, and this is why we choose those theories that refer to what is archaic (Mahler, 1968) and to the theory of "containing" (Bion, 1962a), so that we may reach the parents' own fantasy world.

Phenomenological aspects

The therapist has to establish the parameters of her stability, presence and absence, interaction, language, and working through which space, time, and facts connect. The initial processing (which can last for a very long time) of the parents' discourse is usually mainly phenomenological: the parents must learn to observe what is apparent in their children's behaviour and to be able to describe it. This may be difficult, as at the beginning of their meetings with the therapist the parents have either nothing to say about their child because they are overwhelmed by the emptiness of his psychic world, or they repeat some stereotypic images that hide the emptiness that stems from the child. These stereotypic images may also be massive representations of the parents' own unconscious scenarios, which, because of their primitiveness and lack of secondary working through, cannot be processed by the therapist in such a way as to show the parents their deeper meaning. There are some scenarios that are unconsciously evoked in parents' distortions of their child's sometimes violent play; such scenarios are linked to a thought that the child possesses some monstrously destructive tendencies. For instance, a parent of a very young child once said: "He is capable of taking apart the whole house, destroying everything and everybody." If the therapist were to interpret such a fantasy as projection of the parent towards the child, she would probably be correct, but her aim would be wrong because such an interpretation would not find its way to be integrated into the parent's mental world. The therapist can, instead, use a mythological or a fairy-tale metaphor or even a joke—"You are telling me that your child is like the terrible dragons of fairy tales." Then, through partial regression, the parents may begin to feel that their fear is magnified, and thus a path may be opened to their own childish world of fantasy.

Progress in cooperation:
identifications and fantasies

The therapist, in her attempt to repair external reality and the way this is integrated into inner psychic reality in which the interaction between the child and his parents takes place, collects all the details of everyday life as parts of a jigsaw puzzle and is obliged to construct the parts that are missing. This constructive activity, which is taking place in front of the parents, is extremely useful and sometimes extremely urgent; for instance, when the therapist has to face repetitive self-aggressive or even self-traumatic activity of the child, as in the case of skin-peeling or hand-biting, connected with parent–child interaction. These constructions should be communicated to the parents, always taking care to give them the impression that they are themselves participating in the thought process. Otherwise, the therapist is idealized and the parents are infantilized and become dependent on a therapist who, as an omnipotent object, can be felt by the parents as overprotective; however, she may at the same time be felt as persecutory through a sudden alteration. If and when these difficulties of archaic origin are avoided, mental-constructive attempts for understanding and making sense should be undertaken with caution because parents, by identifying with the therapist, may be led to tend continuously to explain everything in an obsessive way. This pathological behaviour, from which, unfortunately, some inexperienced professionals are not excluded, is a continuous violence towards the other person, who is bombarded by interpretations; it is also a distortion of psychic processes of the therapist herself as she does not allow for silence, which can serve as the mental pause that will enhance the emergence of thoughts and fantasies. Behind the professionals' and the parents' words, the great fear of emptiness, which is motivated by the encounter with psychosis, is hidden. It is at this emptiness that the therapeutic interventions described in the previous sections are aimed in an effort to structure it through the production of representations in the child, the parents, the family, at home, and at school. The representations/connections/interpretations of thoughts, feelings, and fantasies form the bridging, fortification, and drainage of the violence produced by psychotic pathology and provide an economical way of dealing with it.

However, the real therapeutic alliance at which we aim when working with parents is not based on the healthy parts of the personality of the child and of his parents. These parts form very useful interacting units, but the real structuring will be realized— if it can ever be realized—on the pathological parts of the personality. In order to be able to perceive them, we must create the opportunity for them to be sufficiently expressed. This means that the active attitude of the therapist should be accompanied by an attitude that can be described as a "non-interventionist expectation". This will help the therapist endure the emergence of "paradoxical" or "mad" elements that will appear during silence and

feelings of emptiness. This particular condition is especially obvious in sessions in which the child participates, but it is also present
in the discourse of the parents in most of their interviews with the
therapist. The fact that the therapist can endure this "madness"
without letting her capacity to think be destroyed, and without
breaking down through depression or resorting to actings, serves
as a model for the parents of the ways they could face their children's pathology through imitating and eventually identifying
with the therapist. The parents can, perhaps, decrease their own
multiple actings—that is, violent interruption of the child's activity
or even physical violence. The fact that the therapist can tolerate
what sounds as "mad" and can also tolerate acts with which she
does not agree serves as a model; most importantly, this keeps the
parents far away from the psychotic condition which cannot endure antitheses as it uses splittings, thus dividing everything into
"either black or white", or, in psychoanalytic terms, exclusively
persecutory or exclusively protective part-objects. If the parents
feel that the therapist can tolerate such splittings, this can contribute to the setting-in of a condition that Klein (1935) has termed
the "depressive position"—that is, parents, child, and therapist
can from now on be experienced as "good" and "bad" at the same
time.

Depressive position and guilt

The establishment of a working condition as far removed as
possible from the problems of splitting moves the parents away
from the feeling that they are judged by the therapist and per-
mits the setting-in of critical thought and the processing of their
unconscious and latent guilt that tends to be expressed. We are
not referring to conscious guilt, which all parents suffer from and
which they express systematically by trying to compensate
through the sometimes excessive care they provide for their child.
We are referring to unconscious guilt that is connected with important aggression towards the child. The therapist should be aware of
these aggressive movements and should try to discuss them with
the parents, interpreting this as a tendency to attack and kill that
aims not at the child but at his "illness". If this basic psychic move-

ment does not surface, the therapist will be continuously faced with parents' aggressive acts towards the child but also towards the therapeutic setting, which is felt by the parents as either a deposit of the child's disturbance or an idealized therapist–saviour who remains idle and does not "exorcize evil".

Libidinal and aggressive investments

The professional staff working with the parents, but also other members of the institution—that is, special educators, child therapists, scientific and administrative staff—should be sensitive to any manifestation of the parents' aggression even when this is latent or expressed in a passive way, such as in cases of parents who systematically bring the child late to school, or do not inform the staff about important events of family life, or even when the parents or the child are frequently absent without any valid excuse, and so on. Any delay in dealing with such disguised aggressive tendencies could lead to an escalation, and therapists will sometimes realize it when it is too late—for instance, when parents suddenly withdraw the child from the therapeutic setting. This abrupt removal of the child from the therapeutic setting and from persons with whom the child has formed a meaningful relationship could be very destructive for the child, for his progress and development. Another example of such aggressive acts is when parents bring the child to PERIVOLAKI in the morning but enrol him simultaneously for the afternoon in another therapeutic setting with an educational orientation that is incompatible with our own—settings that use behaviour-modification techniques based on classical learning theory, or where the child starts traditional language therapy, not modified for autistic or psychotic children.

Although the parents' aggressive tendencies should be quickly recognized and processed, it is not useful to interpret their libidinal-erotic tendencies towards the therapist; the professional should be able to recognize these tendencies in order to turn them towards the parent–child relation. This means that the therapist should keep a safe distance both from the demands and from the material that the parents bring to the session; she should be able to listen with interest and offer her own thoughts as complementary to the parents', but she should not project elements from her own personality in discussion with them. The session should be conducted as if the therapist were to "vaccinate" the parents with her own libidinal investment to thought processes and to the therapy of psychosis, since she has herself chosen this area of work. The therapist should be effaced as an individual in order to allow the parents to incorporate a way by which they could interact with their child. It should be stressed that not only the professionals working with the parents but all members of the staff of the institution should adopt a similar attitude towards the parents so as not to encourage any seductive tendencies the parents may have towards them.

It is also most important that the institution does not encourage seductive tendencies that the professional staff may have towards the parents. It is preferable that the institution is presented to the parents as one solution among others, a solution that the parents themselves have chosen for their child, with the emphasis actually put upon the fact that it is a mutual choice, which can be modified or even cease. If the institution presents itself as the "perfect" or "unique" solution, then the parents' symbiotic, adhesive, or addictive tendencies will be reinforced and the parents will be infantilized. They will remain immature and unable to organize their family's life and the progress of therapies, while at the same time the child's enrolment and adaptation will be hampered as the parents will remain attached to the omnipotent setting.

* * *

The following vignette illustrates the way we think of the parents' acts and psychic movements.

"Celestine"

The parents had originally denied Celestine's early problems, and for four years they tried, without success, to enrol her in regular schools.* They finally decided to bring her to PERIVOLAKI

---

*We chose the name "Celestine" for this case to stress the impression this child gave us at times—as without real substance and dark, like a cloudy sky.

at the age of 8 years. During the preliminary diagnostic phase, we noticed that the mother had a psychotic nucleus with false-self defences and a symbiotic relation with her daughter. The father had a chronic latent depression against which he used impulsive hyperactivity with regard to external reality— for example, excessive work and frequent change of direction of professional activities—and psychosomatic dysfunction or even illnesses with regard to internal psychic reality.

Celestine used to hide her face and gaze from under her hair, and she spoke very slowly, often in a special imaginary dialogue with her mother—for example, "Do it, little Cecil" or, "I am going to tear her up, I will cut you into pieces" (her mother used a diminutive form of her name). Celestine was originally allowed to regress at PERIVOLAKI and was taken care of psychologically and somatically. After some time, she began to trust the school, the teachers, and her psychotherapist and made important progress in interpersonal relations and in her participation in classroom activities. Her language had improved, but her voice was often effacing. We hypothesized that as Celestine was relating with her mother in a symbiotic way, she experienced the use of language as if putting some distance between them, a distance she could not tolerate, hence the effacing voice.

The family therapist tried to help the mother to put some distance between herself and Celestine and to allow the child to express her individuality. The mother tried at times to keep that distance, but in spite of her efforts not to control Celestine, she very often kept her in a tight and very severe embrace. If Celestine showed any sign of independence or disobedience, the mother kept her at home for a couple of days and told us that the child did not want to come to school. On the other hand, Celestine, being unable to find a way out of this tight embrace, developed constipation, a fact that increased her dependence upon the mother but also increased the mother's possibility of exerting violence on her (through enemas). This vicious circle was repeated several times before the family therapist and the mother could start to discuss it.

Another way in which the mother controlled the child was to keep the child at home with the slightest excuse—for example, she feared another child at school might hit Celestine. When the mother was ill, she also kept the child at home. We then decided to see mother and child together, told them that they were two different people, and asked the mother to state clearly to Celestine that she wished her to come to school every day. Celestine returned to school and continued regular attendance for some time.

As Celestine grew up, her parents realized that she suffered from a chronic illness, and this created a lot of anxiety. At that time, after discussion with them, we suggested individual psychotherapy for the mother (which she did not accept) and, at the same time, helped the family to organize afternoon activities (ballet and music) for Celestine in groups with less disturbed children. Unfortunately, the father used his professional overactivity and his psychosomatic illness to keep at distance from the mother–child dyad; he was also absent from the couple therapy sessions. The mother tended to create in fantasy a couple of herself and the family therapist, a couple that had the characteristics of a relation with a "double" and in which all elements of alterity were lost for the mother. Realizing that it would take a long time for the therapist to work through this difficult situation, we tried to enhance the child's relation with an aunt in order to introduce a third person within this highly symbiotic relationship. Celestine showed spectacular progress: she became more independent and started asking for individual meetings with members of the unit; she used symbolic play, spoke more loudly, expressed some personal thoughts and wishes, showed her anger, and, most importantly, started to get angry with her mother; and she also started to read and write.

After the summer holiday when Celestine was aged 12½ years and could still stay at the unit for another two school years, the mother—probably through a psychic movement that entailed psychotic disorganization (during the summer the father had a serious cardiac episode and was hospitalized; when he returned, he refused the help offered by the mother and started working again)—acted out by not bringing Celestine to school once or twice a week, without explaining to the staff the reason for the child's absences. In a highly emotional meeting between the mother and the case supervisor, she announced that she had organized a "scenario speech therapy" for Celestine at home, that if Celestine went to ordinary school at the age of 14 years (the age at which the children leave the unit) everybody would start thinking, "Who is that tall person wandering about?" The mother also said: "It is as if this child has two brains, one crazy and the other normal", that "Celestine needs a whole pie, whereas here at Perivolaki you only give her little bits and pieces", and that she had decided to give her the whole pie at home, which is why she would stop bringing the child to school.

We thought that the mother's words were indicative of the way that she thought and felt about her child. The "tall person wandering about" represents the realization of Celestine's chronic condition. She has grown up but still cannot do what other children of her age do. The mother's hopes for a more "normal" development tended to evaporate, and this was a strong blow to her narcissism. The "scenario speech therapy" that the mother thought she was going to offer to Celestine updated her conviction (which most parents have) that if the child could express her thoughts verbally, then all problems would end. At the same time, this was a hint against PERIVOLAKI, since we resist any requests for conventional speech therapy. The mother's idea that the child had "two brains, one crazy and one normal" was a projection of the mother's representation of herself: (a) one conscious, which was the part of her false self that related with the external world in a conservative and consenting way, and (b) one unconscious, which was the archaic part of herself that pushed her to repetition. This split was also her effort to exorcise the bad part of the child and at the same time preserved her hope that the child might have a healthy part in her brain. Hope such as this is very important for the therapist–parent alliance, although there may be some risk of parents becoming very demanding towards the child. The idea of the "split brain" may also lead parents in an endless investigation for a biological answer for the child's condition, which stands against more psychological ways of looking into it. Finally, the "whole pie" meant that Celestine needed only what her omnipotent mother possessed, whereas PERIVOLAKI had only "bits and pieces". The mother expressed this idea the moment she realized that the child would soon have to go away from PERIVOLAKI, which had up to then been protective but could not go on providing for them forever. This showed the mother's incapacity to accept the idea of boundaries and the feeling of frustration, as she had not incorporated into her mental apparatus the concept of castration. She consequently projected her frustration to external reality; she imposed a condition of castration and mourning on PERIVOLAKI while she herself retired with her daughter in an illusory omnipotent symbiotic circle.

Project of work—project of life

PERIVOLAKI, with its organized life, programmes its own development and activities and evaluates the progress of each child every year; this gives the parents the message that working for the therapy of psychotic children has a meaning and may be effective for some people (professionals) since there are projects for further development. Any such project that will be continuously modified according to the child's progress should be among the central points of discussion in the sessions with the parents so that they can invest in this project mentally and emotionally.

The construction of such a project has a very basic foundation: that of "body image". The child presents himself to his parents and to the professionals in a fragmented way through his behaviour, but he must be represented in a unified scheme at every stage of his development by the professional staff and by his parents. This could be enhanced through a description that defines his psychosomatic function, a function that is very different from the anatomical and mental functions of other children of his age (Alexandridis, 1990, 1997). For instance, if we ask ourselves or the parents the question, "How do you think the child imagines himself?", the reply might be for one child that he is like a mouth trying all kinds of tastes and experiences, or for another child that he is like a tube that can hold nothing inside, or for yet another one that he is like a scratched surface which seeks a protective skin by trying to attach himself onto others. The imaging of the child is of paramount importance for autistic children, and for many years it is perhaps the best level of comprehension the parents can reach. For psychotic children, and especially for those among them who have developed language to a relatively adequate level, the imaging of the child is easier for the professionals, as it can be based and built on the child's spoken language. It is, however, much more difficult for the parents to create such a representation, as their child is motivated by primitive and non-elaborated narcissistic, homosexual, and incestuous fantasies, which, if presented or discussed with the parents, will evoke anxiety and abomination. Consequently, the therapist will have to interpret such hypotheses only for herself and will eventually relate her thoughts about the type of the child's fantasies to other members of the team of professionals that handles the case of each family. Meanwhile, the therapist should try to find the right kind of counsel for everyday life to offer to the parents. Such counselling could be in the form of interpretation equivalents so that the child's unconscious fantasies are partially satisfied. For instance, suppose that a child dashes his head forcibly and repeatedly against his mother's stomach. The symptom annoys the whole family. The family therapist working with the parents will ask them to inform the child's therapist. The latter may interpret the symptom to the child as a wish to return to the womb by aggressively penetrating it; as she is bound by client confidentiality, she will not communicate her thoughts to the parents, but she can assure them that she will try to talk about it with the child. The family therapist, who most probably will have similar thoughts about the child's symptom, will not discuss them with the parents because of the violence they could motivate. She can only discuss with the parents the child's probable desire of return to the womb; she may even suggest to them that they talk to the child about the time his mother was pregnant with him and how both parents were discussing it, how they imagined he would be after he was born. The family therapist may also suggest to the mother that she play a game with the child, wrapping her dress around him—that is, to play a sort of pregnancy/birth game—or even suggest that they play the game with dolls, if the child is able to symbolize through play.

The family therapist is thus inspired from basic primary process and expresses formulations using secondary process to suggest to the parents things to do with their child. The therapist is thus symbolizing on their behalf some things that they cannot symbolize themselves. In many cases, parents appropriate the therapist's thinking, and this leads to an amelioration that helps the whole family's functioning—not only towards the sick child, but between the couple and towards the other children of the family. Especially if there are younger children in the family, the parents' work with a specialist can play the role of early prognosis, prevention, and intervention. The dangerous consequences of the multiply loaded burden created by the chronic condition of living with a psychotic sibling are thus diminished. The justified anxiety of the parents for the development of younger siblings of their psychotic child is also diminished, and the family can to some extent detach its happiness from the very slow progress of the sick child's pathology. The present can be invested as a time span that can be happy and creative. The ability to live the here-and-now without excessive anxiety and to be able to form a concept of "present time" is perhaps a victory of paramount importance *vis-à-vis* psychosis, the emblem of which is denial and fragmentation of actual external and internal reality.

CHAPTER SIX

Working with parents of autistic children

Didier Houzel

Over the years since psychoanalytic treatment of early infantile autism was first attempted, a rift has opened between the parents of autistic children and psychoanalysis. There are many reasons for this, but I believe that the principal factor is the misuse of psychoanalysis in this area, together with a lack of conceptual and methodological rigour. I would argue that it is necessary to reflect on these points if we are to establish a new kind of productive dialogue between parents and therapists. It seems paradoxical that psychoanalysis, with its emphasis on understanding and help, should be experienced as a threat and set aside as a heavy and useless encumbrance. This paradox, it seems to me, has many lessons for us, in the same way that other theoretical or technical stumbling-blocks mark the frontiers of our present knowledge yet may also herald new advances.

I think that, up to a point, the situation of infantile autism over the last thirty years can be compared to the predicament that medical science found itself in at the end of the last century with respect to hysteria and the adult neuroses in general. At that time, neurology, with its emphasis on the systematic study of nerve paths and on an ever more thorough knowledge of the anatomy of the central nervous system, was faced with an enigma: the symptoms of hysterical conversion. Brain lesions could explain observed symptomatology by means of the anatomical and functional mapping between nerve lesion and peripheral manifestation, but hysterical symptoms did not lend themselves to any kind of comprehensible systematization. Thus hysteria was a challenge to the medical practitioners of the time—it was all Greek to them—and as a result they were quickly to become exasperated by these unclassifiable and baffling patients. From then on, there has been a kind of permanent divorce between somatic medicine and the patient who suffers from hysteria.

This was to be Freud's starting point (1895d). The decisive progress he made in the understanding of hysteria—and of the neuroses as a whole—was due to the fact that he was able to move away from the established idea according to which each and every sensorimotor malfunction could be explained by a lesion of a controlling nerve centre or pathway. Freud was thereupon in a position to discover that the *meaning*, if not the explanation, of conversion symptoms lay in the individual's past, particularly in his early childhood, through his conscious and, even more to the point, unconscious relationships with significant others in his immediate circle during his first years of life. For Freud, if neurological symptoms could be traced back to an impairment of the anatomical and functional integrity of the nervous system, neurotic symptoms on the other hand had to be referred to what W. R. Bion (1961) was to call *an intelligible field of study*, that of the unconscious relationships established between the individual and those in close contact with him. The meaning of symptoms was no longer to be discovered within the individual *per se*, but in the relationships developed between him and his objects.

This was the starting point for psychoanalysts when they began to explore infantile autism and the psychopathology of early childhood. They found themselves, *mutatis mutandis*, in a position comparable to that of the nineteenth-century neurologists—they had a theoretical model and a technique of investigation that worked well for certain disorders, but when these were transposed to another type of pathology they proved not only ineffective but also sometimes harmful. In retrospect, the reason for this seems clear enough: the psychoanalytic exploration of child psychopathology gave rise to confusion in many minds between people in the child's real life, in particular his parents, and those in his internal world. The discovery that autistic children suffer from massive anxiety and have tremendous difficulty in feeling any kind of inner security led some practitioners to blame the child's parents for being the source of that anxiety or the cause of the difficulty.

It should be borne in mind that Kanner himself, who was not a psychoanalyst, concluded his seminal paper on early infantile autism with a fairly scathing description of the parents of autistic children he had met, and he remained somewhat equivocal as to their responsibility in the development of their child's mental state:

> In the whole group, there are very few warm-hearted fathers and mothers. For the most part, the parents, grandparents, and collaterals are persons strongly preoccupied with abstractions of a scientific, literary, or artistic nature, and limited in genuine interest in people. Even some of the happiest marriages are rather cold and formal affairs. Three of the marriages were dismal failures. The question arises whether or to what extent this fact has contributed to the condition of the children. [Kanner, 1943, p. 42]

This passage has had serious repercussions on the history and understanding of infantile autism, as well as on the treatment of the disorder. Kanner himself, however, tried to diminish its impact by immediately counterbalancing his judgement on parental responsibility: "The children's aloneness from the beginning of life makes it difficult to attribute the whole picture exclusively to the type of the early parental relations with our patients" (p. 42). A little later in the same paper, and in contradiction to what he had just written, he suggests that the syndrome he is describing may have a constitutional aetiology:

> We must, then, assume that these children have come into the world with an innate inability to form the usual, biologically-provided affective contact with people, just as other children come into the world with innate physical or intellectual handicaps. [pp. 42–43]

So there it is: the autistic child suffers from some constitutional disability, hence there is no meaning to be found in his behaviour, in his bizarre contact and communication, or in his sometimes absent, sometimes explosive emotional reactions. A careful scrutiny of Kanner's paper reveals that his conclusions can only be described as surprising. The body of his text is rigorously precise, a model of clinical description, yet his concluding remarks, both as to the judgement passed on parents and as to his biological hypotheses, have no clinical or methodological foundation whatsoever. The impression is that Kanner was bowing to the custom of the time which no doubt demanded that any paper on psychopathology should end with hypotheses or even affirmations as to aetiology. When he discovered the sheer amount of speculation—biological and psychogenetic—that his text had sparked off, Kanner retreated to a more cautious position—but it is much more difficult to distance oneself *post hoc* from hasty conclusions than it is to avoid them in the first place. Though he tried in vain to claim that he had always defended mothers against accusations that they were the cause of the psychopathological disorders of their offspring, his statements of 1943 remained firmly attached to the image that psychiatrists had of the parents of autistic children, even though, as I have said, Kanner did not put forward any direct evidence to support his claim.

Back to the point, which is the role of psychoanalysis. It has to be acknowledged that many psychoanalysts had not fully understood that if psychoanalysis describes pathogenic relationships between a patient and other people, these are fantasy relationships and not historically accurate ones: the *dramatis personae* belong to his internal world and not to external reality. As a result of this misunderstanding, child psychoanalysis has often been little more than a reactive and trauma-based model of child psychopathology. This again is paradoxical, for a great deal of Freud's theoretical effort was put into constructing psychogenetic models that would *not* be seen as reactive. The fact that a given event may give rise to abnormal mental reactions is a mere truism; the fact that certain existential trauma (I am thinking here more specifically of child sexual abuse, physical mistreatment, and neglect) may bring about personality and emotional disorders was acknowledged well before psychoanalysis existed, and, unfortunately, it remains true to this day, even in the developed countries. But the whole point is that Freud's models make no direct reference to such pathogenic factors. What Freud demonstrated was that whatever the external circumstances of the individual, in particular during childhood—the period when the development of mind becomes organized—certain kinds of conflict and suffering, which may indeed give rise to psychopathological gridlock, exist because of the very operation of the internal dynamics that govern development. Traumatic life-events may well facilitate such gridlock, but they are not to be thought of as the aetiological basis of mental disorder. In putting forward this theory, Freud created what the French philosopher Gaston Bachelard called an "epistemological fracture" (Bachelard, 1972).

From that point on, nothing would ever be the same again. Henceforth, psychopathology was looked at in a new light as something that is played out on another stage, answering to a different logic, another causality. In substance, it is no longer a matter of discovering the aetiology of symptoms but their *meaning*—in other words, not where they come from, but where they lead to. The problem in itself was well known to the philosophers, who, from ancient Greece on, had discussed different sorts of causality. Aristotle, for example, differentiates between final causes and efficient causes, and this division was adopted by the scholastics. Efficient causes are those that impart momentum to observed phenomenon, prefacing it as an antecedent. Natural science has to do with efficient causality; in medicine, for example, it lies at the heart of the concept of aetiology. Final causes designate what the observed phenomenon aims for—"sense", and I would stress that this word involves both the idea of meaning and that of direction. Psychoanalysis has to do with final causes, meanings, and not with efficient causes, aetiology.

It is well known that, while he was a student at university, Freud was introduced to this kind of philosophical speculation by the great Aristotelian philosopher Franz Brentano, whose lectures Freud attended in Vienna. Brentano taught a philosophy of intentionality, drawing a distinction between objects in the real world and psychic phenomena. For Brentano (1874), what differentiates physical from psychic phenomena is not a difference in kind, as Descartes claimed, but a difference in intent: physical phenomena refer to efficient causes, psychic phenomena to final causes. For reasons too complex to go into here, Brentano rejected the hypothesis of the unconscious, and this is probably why Freud makes no explicit mention of him in his theoretical texts. It is, however, quite clear that Freud takes up the idea of intentionality, though he applies it not only to conscious psychic phenomena but also to unconscious ones. The Freudian unconscious could be defined as that which tends towards thought processes that lie outside the field of consciousness. Brentano's intent becomes Freud's "cathexis" [*Besetzung*], which could be defined as an unconscious intentionality.

With these postulates in mind, let us now explore what is at stake in the psychotherapist's work with the parents of an autistic child. In a nutshell, it consists in inviting them to speculate on the meaning of their child's symptoms and to support them in their search for meaning. This has nothing to do with accusations or making them feel guilty. Indeed, if we are to succeed in leading them onto this difficult path, we have to be convinced in our heart of hearts that, no matter how severe the child's disorder, no matter how dysfunctional the relationship between him and his immediate circle, the family is not the cause of his disorder. We will simply have to resign ourselves, once and for all, to abandoning the psychogenetic model of aetiology. On that basis, I now intend to examine the following aspects of the therapist's work with parents: the therapeutic alliance, deciphering the child's emotional expression, assessment of the child's progress, and working through what I will call the parents' *paradoxical depression*.

The therapeutic alliance

The concept of therapeutic alliance was formulated in 1956 by E. Zetzel to designate that part of the patient's transference which is used not as a defensive compromise, but to support the phasing-in of true analytical work. It was taken up again in 1967 by R. R. Greenson under the name *working alliance*. The psychoanalysts who found it necessary to define these concepts worked with adult patients. I have suggested elsewhere (Houzel, 1986) that the concept should be extended to child analysis and include the child's parents. In that paper, I defined the therapeutic alliance as the agreement to enter into a new kind of experience, with its emotional, imaginary, and symbolic aspects, thereby obtaining a glimpse of another way in which the mind can work, different from that to which we are accustomed; it includes also the possibility as well as the hope of making sense of symptoms and mental pain.

I shall not at present discuss in detail the therapeutic alliance with the autistic child himself, given that there are obvious specific problems linked to the fact that, generally speaking, the autistic child is unable to give his agreement in any explicit way. I shall therefore concentrate on the therapeutic alliance with the child's parents.

The alliance is established during the preliminary meetings, at least some of which, in my opinion, should be used for seeing parents and child together. In the course of these meetings, the consultant or psychotherapist should, with due respect for parental narcissism, attempt to highlight possible meanings in the child's autistic manifestations. The following is an example of what I mean:

This is my second consultation with a 2-year-old autistic girl, "Aline". I had seen her once before with both parents present. On this second occasion, when I come into the waiting-room for her, she seems relaxed and signals clearly that she recognizes me (sitting on her mother's lap, she leans over towards me, as though inviting me to take her into my arms). At that moment, she does not in the least appear autistic. Yet almost as soon as we enter the consulting-room, Aline becomes absorbed, in a very autistic manner, in contemplating one of her hands which she is waving in front of her face. I realize then that we are not in an identical situation to the previous one: this time, Aline's father is absent. He was to make his own way to the consultation, but he is late and we have begun the meeting without him. I comment along these lines on what is happening: I say to Aline and her mother that Aline is no doubt glad to see me again, but it is upsetting for her when we are together without her daddy. The father arrives a few minutes later; as soon as he is in the room, Aline stops contemplating her hand and holds her arms out towards her father.

This very straightforward example illustrates the kind of work that can be done in the preliminary meetings to help parents realize that their child's autistic symptoms are not devoid of relational meaning and, therefore, that psychotherapeutic work is worth while. It then becomes possible to satisfy their legitimate curiosity and explain to them what the psychotherapy planned for their child involves. I usually tell them that it consists in helping their child gradually to understand his innermost feelings and to show him that other people too can understand them, share them, and communicate them; this in turn may help him to overcome obstacles to growth, because once things can be communicated they lose their power to disorganize and to cause distress.

A true therapeutic alliance with the parents can be agreed upon once they themselves have witnessed attempts at understanding through interpretations and commentaries, as I have shown above. This does not, of course, mean that there will be no manifestations of resistance on their part as the therapy proceeds. As the child makes progress in therapy, the therapeutic alliance needs to be reinforced by means of regular assessment meetings. I do nonetheless emphasize the importance of an initial alliance with the parents to serve as a reference point that will prove to be particularly useful whenever the road ahead seems too long, the outcome too uncertain, and misgivings, discouragement, or even depression loom.

Deciphering the child's emotional expression

I do not hold with the hypothesis according to which autistic children are incapable of emotional expression or empathy with others. This hypothesis forms part of the model proposed by Leslie and Frith (1988) and is based on the concept of a theory of mind. According to this model, which purports to explain why autistic children are unable to communicate with their immediate circle,

they do not have a theory of mind—that is, they have no representation of what the other person may feel, imagine, desire, or think.
There is much cognitive research to support this hypothesis, but
there are two ways in which the findings can be interpreted. The
first is that of Leslie and Frith, who claim aetiological implications:
the autistic child has a constitutional deficit in the neurological
equipment necessary for developing a theory of mind. The second
possible interpretation has defensive connotations: in interpersonal relationships, the autistic child feels threatened with such
devastating psychic disorganization that his only way of escape is
to avoid any such intersubjective communication altogether—
hence the retreat from physical contact, avoidance of eye-contact,
and non-development of communication skills, which include not
only language but also deciphering of emotions and non-verbal
communication. The absence of a theory of mind is seen in this
case to be the consequence of these forced avoidance procedures,
which therefore could be thought of as defence mechanisms
against psychic disorganization and anxiety.

This second perspective makes it easier to understand the emotional manifestations of autistic children. They may be enigmatic,
but they are intense and sometimes even violent—a far cry from
the absence of emotional reaction implied by the constitutional-
deficit theory. Autistic children seem to be locked in a struggle
against their own emotions. Their avoidance behaviour can be
construed as a strategy for evading situations that might trigger
an emotion, along the same lines as their concern for preservation
of sameness, which Kanner (1943) himself emphasized. If nothing
changes, if we avoid all encounters, if we live in a world without
history, without a partner, without communication, then we
maximize our chances of suppressing all inner movement—our
emotions, which, in seeking expression, drive the mind towards a
goal, towards personal encounters, towards something new to be
explored and understood.

The reason for avoidance of emotions remains to be discussed.
In my view, the autistic child's emotions, far from being absent or
negligible, are extremely powerful, but he does not know how to
hold them in check or to organize them in such a way that they
become comprehensible to his immediate circle, which can then

share them with him. The autistic child's emotions present themselves as an instantaneous and uncontrollable flood. Externally, this is evidenced in two ways: either through outbursts of stereotyped motor movements that appear to be an ultimate desperate attempt to regain control over something that he feels is about to overwhelm him, or through violent explosions of anger, mingled with anxiety, that bewilder both the child and his family because they seem so out of proportion to the external situation.

I think it very important to grasp these external signs in order to try to decipher the emotion the child is feeling and to talk to him about it in simple terms and in words he can understand—thereby encouraging him to participate in human communication, which is based above all on sharing experiences of states of mind. Any child who finds himself filled with emotion normally has to share it immediately with those around him: he rushes up to his mother, for example, to share with her his sorrows and his joys. As soon as he learns to talk, he uses language not so much to exchange information as to relate, to comment on, and to share his states of mind. It is only gradually that language becomes a vehicle for transmitting information in a more objective manner, and even then this is never entirely the case. The child's motivation for learning to talk is, above all, the fact that he then becomes able to share and to explore through interpersonal communication his own states of mind and those of other people. This is what the autistic child cannot cope with, which is why he has to be helped to make this discovery.

In this, the parents play the role of co-therapists. They are, after all, the day-to-day witnesses of their child's reactions in any given situation; they know precisely how his states of mind are signalled—how he shows he feels relaxed, worried, angry, and so forth. They may need the consultant's help in order to decipher these signals more accurately and to put them into words. Here is a brief example of what I mean:

> "Alain" is 9 years old and has been in psychoanalytic psychotherapy for the past five years, with four sessions per week. He was severely autistic at the beginning of his analysis, but he has since made considerable progress. His speech is normal, he attended nursery school and now attends primary school,

having had to repeat only one class. He still, however, concerns himself with matters that bear little relationship to the actual situation, and his speech is often submerged by repetitive themes to do with these concerns of his. He is a good example of what Meltzer has called "post-autistic states" (Meltzer et al., 1975).

One day his mother agreed at a moment's notice to stand in for another mother who was due to accompany Alain's class on a school outing to see a show. Alain was very upset and disruptive all through the show: he threw himself on the floor and picked bits of fuzz from the carpet instead of watching the various acts. As they left, Alain's mother said something to him in a reproachful tone, expressing her disappointment: she had expected him to be delighted that she was coming along. Alain answered in an extremely depressed voice, saying that he hadn't liked anything, everything had bored him, the bus that was to take them home was very late in arriving, etc. In the discussion I had later with the mother, I stressed the fact that Alain had had no preparation for the last-minute change and had not been expecting his mother to come along. Maybe that had overwhelmed him emotionally, and the only way he could express this was through his disruptive behaviour during the show and his depressed and depressing answer when she spoke to him about it. By helping Alain's mother to understand that all emotions, not only negative ones, were probably overwhelming for Alain, I was able to support her hope of pleasing him by going on the trip.

We have to anticipate the child's emotions if we are to help him enter into the world of communication. He cannot make the first move, for he does not know there is a first move to make. He probably feels himself in the grip of states of mind that are meaningless to him; he does not even know what to call them, and he does not realize that other people can understand them. This kind of deciphering involves intuition, and I always try to encourage parental intuition in this respect. Often, parents have insufficient confidence in their ability to imagine what their child is feeling and expressing, and therefore they hesitate to make use of it. I believe that we should share with them our own uncertainty in this area, as well as our belief that, even if we do make mistakes, the overriding requirement is to propose to the child a deciphered version of what he tells us about his states of mind. This is a fundamental parental function that Bion (1962a) called "the mother's capacity for reverie" or "alpha function".

I have devised an outreach treatment technique to offer parents a significant degree of help and support on this aspect. It is a therapeutic application of Esther Bick's method of infant observation. The therapist visits the family home once or twice a week for one-hourly sessions. The approach is similar to that of baby observers—that is, to show attentiveness and receptivity towards the conscious and unconscious messages addressed to him or her by the child and his family. After each treatment session, detailed notes are made of everything the observer remembers; these notes are then discussed several times per week in workshop meetings in which I participate. This therapeutic method is particularly appropriate for young autistic children who have been diagnosed as such before the age of 3 years, and it offers parents mental support in their task of attending to their child's mental growth and making sense of what they perceive of his states of mind. It is my belief that autistic processes make a powerful attack on parental attentiveness and that it is necessary to help them recover their full capacity in this area, particularly where deciphering their child's emotional expression is concerned.

Assessment of the child's progress

Here, too, there is some degree of reciprocity between the help that parents are offered by the therapist and that which they can give him; the key here, of course, is to avoid role confusion. Regular assessment meetings together are necessary for ensuring that, in their own way, everyone is pulling in the same direction and that this direction is the correct one. These assessment meetings are indispensable, too, for mutual support. Another aim is to evaluate the work that lies ahead and to discuss what new measures fall to be taken as the occasion arises, both as to the treatment itself and as to other kinds of assistance that might help the child (educational or day-to-day care, for example).

One of the difficulties that parents encounter is how to decide on appropriate criteria for assessing their child's progress. Let me describe my own experience in this domain. In general, parents begin by saying that there is no improvement at all: "He's just the same as before, or maybe even worse!" Then they go on to describe what they feel has changed and improved. The end result, after an hour's discussion of the changes they have in fact observed, is usually that there are some quite significant signs of real progress. Why, then, the contrast between an initially disenchanted assessment and the highly positive end result? I believe that the problem is one of choosing appropriate criteria. If the assessment is based on normative developmental criteria—for example, the child's speech has not improved much, his learning ability is still quite limited, and so on—disappointment is understandable. On the other hand, what may have happened is that contact and communication with him are better, his emotions are easier to identify, from time to time he has calm spells during which he seems thoughtful, and there is even some elementary pretend-play. Parents (and, later, teachers) have to be helped to change their assessment criteria and move away from developmental norms towards signs of improved communication and mental functioning.

There are two main reasons why change of criteria is important. The first is that to expect a child who, because of his autism, is years behind in many areas of development to move closer and closer to established norms is probably unrealistic; actual results can only be thoroughly despairing and depressing. Parental expectations are quite understandable. It would mean a great deal to parents if their child could simply erase the discontinuities between chronological age, cognitive capacity, and behaviour—all the more so since these children are usually in good physical health, so that there is no obvious reason for such discrepancies to exist. Parents have to be helped to appreciate the true value of certain aspects of development that most rating scales ignore, aspects that are highly significant for intersubjective communication and intrapsychic growth. This is a crucial step in supporting the efforts put in by parents and therapists alike. It is impossible to undertake such a long and mentally arduous adventure—therapy with an autistic child—without from time to time verifying that some developmental stages have been attained and that things are moving in the right direction.

The second reason for modifying assessment criteria is that the autistic child is highly sensitive to the expectations he feels that adults in his environment have of him. The more he feels that they are hoping for a given improvement, performance, or achievement, the more difficult it is for him to respond. If expectations are too high and too relentless, they produce the opposite effect from the one hoped for and put a brake on progress rather than facilitate it. It is as though the child can feel on his shoulders the whole weight of these hopes, with the result that his anxiety and inhibition increase. This is one of the major difficulties that parents and therapists have to cope with: hope for the child to make progress, stimulate him towards improvement, do everything in their power to help him grow—yet at the same time not count on immediate tangible results and not expect progress to permit objective assessment. The autistic child spends some considerable time in learning things in a roundabout way rather than directly, and he demonstrates his achievements tangentially—and usually when we least expect them.

Working with paradoxical depression in parents

One of the more surprising discoveries I have made in my work with parents of autistic children is the advent of a sometimes severe depressive reaction just when, in my view, the psychotherapeutic process is beginning to bear fruit and produce results. This kind of reaction is what I call *paradoxical depression*. It is mainly encountered in mothers, in my experience, but sometimes fathers can suffer from it too. This is usually the way the situation arises: as the child's therapist, I am happy with the way he is progressing; he appears to be communicating more and really beginning to work things out in his mind. Yet, contrary to all expectations, the parents complain that the situation is worse than ever and that their child is so difficult that they just cannot take any more. They appear to be on the brink of utter despondency. When I first encountered this kind of parental depressive reaction, I found it difficult to understand; I had to make the effort to think through the situation, and this led me to the following hypothesis. As the parents note how their autistic child's mental life has progressed— and often they can chart these developments with surprising accuracy—they can see also just how great a task lies ahead, and they feel overwhelmed at the prospect. Changes occur, but so very slowly; the parents will have to work hard and persevere if they are to help their child towards further growth. Will they have enough energy? Will they be up to the task? Can they be sure that the therapeutic team will not let them down when they are just half-way along the road?

This depressive reaction sometimes seems to be a renewal of a maternal post-partum depression with a similar theme. The depressed mother feels that she is unable to cope with the task that lies ahead, perhaps because she feels disqualified as to her skills as a mother and insufficiently supported by her immediate circle. I must make it clear that there is no accusation here of failure in maternal functioning, which in such circumstances would be not only absurd but also unfounded. Generally speaking, the mother already has very little confidence in her own ability; it would be much better to encourage and endorse her skills as a mother rather than to cast doubt on them. If we take on an accusatory role, all we are doing—without realizing it—is taking the place of an internal figure, a kind of omnipotent maternal superego, which is blocking the mother on her way to motherhood. That is when we fall unconsciously into the trap instead of avoiding it. What we have to do above all is understand and work through these projections of disqualified mother and disqualifying figure in order to forestall that particular pitfall. The phase of paradoxical depression is particularly suitable for working through what the mother, and sometimes both parents, project onto the therapists.

When I am faced with paradoxical depression, I interpret it by saying to the parents: "Though you can acknowledge the fact that your child has progressed, probably you're finding the whole process too slow and any steps forward too microscopic. You can see the size of the task that lies ahead if you are to help him develop as much as he can. All this overwhelms you and makes you doubt your ability to accomplish this task." I add that the therapeutic team as a whole, whom the parents trust, will not let them down but will stand by them for as long as it takes. It is quite usual in these circumstances for the parents to talk of their fears for the distant future: "What will happen in a year's time, or two years from now, or when you will no longer be here, or when we will no longer be around?" In my experience, parental paradoxical depression can spread to the professionals, including therapists, who are involved with the child; this can sometimes lead to premature and inopportune interruptions in treatment which are particularly difficult for the child and his parents to put up with.

Meetings with parents

Working with the parents of autistic children requires an appropriate setting. I offer them monthly meetings, each of which lasts one hour. When the child first comes in for treatment, before beginning his individual psychotherapy, I suggest that we have joint discussions, parents and child together. This is when the preliminary work is done, leading up to the therapeutic alliance. Once the child's individual psychotherapy begins, I suggest that the parents meet me alone, since I feel that having too many meetings as consultant with the child present is not desirable, because of the risk of interference with the transference relationship he has with his therapist.

Discussions with the parents are non-directive. I invite them to tell me whatever they want to about their child. If they so wish, they may also talk about more personal matters, including any problems they may have as a couple. It is, however, very important to be quite clear about what these meetings are and what they are not: they are not intended to be therapeutic discussions with the parents as adults with some specific problem or other, nor do they amount to parental psychotherapy. If these kinds of treatment are envisaged, then the parents should be referred—on their explicit request—to a psychotherapist who is not involved in any way with the team that works with the child. It is the case all too often that parents—reluctantly—find themselves treated as patients, even though they may have expressed no such desire. This kind of situation arises from false alliances, which do the child no good and may even interfere with the parents' ability to fulfil their task.

When I began working with young autistic and psychotic children, in the early 1970s, I still had in mind the model I had inherited: psychopathology in the child must inevitably reflect a personality disorder in one or other of his parents or some parental malfunction. It followed therefore that parental deficiencies and conflicts were to be investigated through their reminiscences. I tended to orient my discussions with parents along those lines, and, much to my dismay, often obtained very little (or even nothing) of any significance. I have explained earlier in this chapter how I moved away from this pseudo-aetiological path, once I realized that it was less and less relevant. I do believe, however, that once any pretence at aetiology is put aside, it is still useful to explore the child's background and past history, the type of relationship that exists between him and his parents, the memories they have of different periods of his life, and so on. All this can further the consultant's and the psychotherapist's understanding and help the parents gain some insight into their child's difficulties. That said, with parents of autistic children, matters are often quite complex.

Too intensive and systematic an exploration into the past history they share with their child is difficult to bear, and most of the time it provides little in the way of references to the child's development. This is not to say that an investigation of this kind is impossible or useless—but it must be conducted differently. We have to be able to show interest in the daily life of the child and his family and in the small details of the difficulties they experience in bringing him up. Every little detail is to some extent meaningful and should be gathered up in much the same way as an archaeologist gathers up every little piece of antique pottery he or she finds, in order later to reunite them, thereby restoring them to their original shape. In the course of subsequent meetings, perhaps as the result of a seemingly insignificant follow-up question, one or other of the parents may provide a more meaningful item. Gathering meaning together in this way is a very slow process and takes place over many a long year.

> After five years of regular monthly meetings, Alain's mother was finally able to talk about her own mother's death, which had occurred when she was four months into the pregnancy. Two years after that, she spoke of how much she had missed her mother's presence beside her when Alain was born and of how she had felt her mother-in-law's comments to be judgemental and disqualifying.

In cases like this, it is as though we are dealing with a slow-motion film, which cannot be speeded up. Probably a systematic hunt for information at the beginning of the treatment would completely by-pass the more significant events and memories. If, at the beginning of Alain's treatment, I had tried to investigate his mother's subjective experience of her pregnancy and post-partum period, I would in all probability have obtained nothing. Yet there is no doubt that what she was able to tell me, after several years of meetings, had had a significant impact on her and on her experience of motherhood.

I believe that it may be useful, for a better understanding of what is at stake here, to mention what I propose to call the *containing function*, with reference to Bion's work on the container (1962a). The containing function has two component parts: gathering together and stabilizing. Each of these aspects is in dialectic interaction with the other. If, when two elements are brought together in the mind, the result is too much turbulence, they will be kept apart until a container is available to bring them together *and* deal with the ensuing turbulence. For Alain's mother, it was as though bringing together in her mind the loss of her mother ("I closed her eyes when I was four months pregnant," she told me), the birth of her baby, and her mother-in-law's attitude, which she had felt to be hostile and disqualifying, had remained impossible for such a long time because it would have generated unbearable turbulence and disorganization. The containing function that the regular meetings provided and my assiduous listening to whatever Alain's parents wanted to say had at last made it possible to bring these experiences together in a way that was no longer threatening but, on the contrary, made sense of the mother's initial experiences with her baby. This was not simply of historical or theoretical interest: after telling me of these memories, the relationship between Alain and his mother improved dramatically.

I believe that if there happens to be a defect in the containing function as I describe it, this has nothing to do with a constitutional deficiency that could be blamed on some or all parents of autistic children. The only reference here must surely be to background history and to the vicissitudes of a unique relationship. The fact that Alain's mother lost her own mother in particularly painful circumstances (she died of cancer), that she had to close her mother's eyes just as she herself was about to become a mother for the first time, that she was unable to find adequate surrogate support in her immediate circle, in particular with her mother-in-law, who, as a competent mother of several children, enjoyed tremendous prestige and personal authority in the family—this is all part of the particular history of a specific pregnancy, birth, and motherhood. If anyone is to be held responsible for creating the risk of infantile autism, then we all should be—parents, collaterals, professionals, we all have a duty to offer the support of our mindfulness to mothers at such a delicate and important moment in their life, and for preparing the psychic birth of the infant in the same careful and caring way as we prepare its physical birth. Contrary to what has often been claimed, by Kanner in particular, mothers of autistic children have never seemed to me to be rejecting, unloving, or emotionally cold and unfeeling. I tend to find them inhibited in their dealings with the infant they have just brought into the world, this wonderful infant who seems so fragile that they are afraid that they might handle it awkwardly and hurt it. What they missed out on at the very beginning of their experience of motherhood was the firm, reassuring support of their immediate circle, encouraging them to trust in their skills as mothers and encouraging the infant to trust in its own potentialities for growth. It falls to us—psychotherapists, consultants, psychotherapeutic teams—to try to take on this task, helped, whenever possible, by our alliance with the child's father.

Conclusion

The aims of parental meetings as I describe them in this chapter are not restricted. I have drawn attention to those that I think are the most appropriate to the situations that both parents and psychotherapists have to cope with in cases of infantile autism. Having an autistic child is such a painful experience that there should be no need to underline the fact that therapists and consultants must show empathy and deep respect for what the child's parents have to deal with. I would, however, like to stress how difficult this work is for the professionals involved and how much they have to feel that the parents trust them. The rift I mentioned in the opening paragraphs of this chapter was, to my mind, the result of the trial-and-error methods more or less inevitable in any new venture. Now that autism no longer seems so completely enigmatic, even though a certain mystery still remains, we are in a better position to understand the echo that it awakens within each of us, for we have all had to answer the fundamental question that it asks: how to reconcile otherness and sharing intimate experiences with those close to us. The challenge, surely, that remains to be taken up is how parents and professionals can come together on that question for the good of the autistic child.

CHAPTER SEVEN

Helping children through treatment of parenting: the model of mother/infant psychotherapy

Bertrand Cramer

It is well known that treating children often means treating parents. This empirical finding, made by many clinicians (Anna Freud, Fraiberg, Katan, Winnicott) has brought about original forms of treatments: family or systemic therapies and parent/child treatments, among which the best known are Mahler's tripartite treatment (with psychotic children: Mahler et al., 1975) and Fraiberg's mother/infant therapies (Fraiberg, 1980). Several therapists have refined parent/infant therapies, each bringing his or her contributions (Cramer, 1995; Hopkins, 1992; Lebovici, 1983; Lieberman, Weston, & Pawl, 1991). In all these approaches, a major focus of therapy is the complex constellation of conflicts, anxieties, defences, ideals, and relationship modes (both internal and externalized) that produce what is often referred to as parenting. Parenting is a way of describing both how parents actually enact their relational and educational competencies with their children, and how they represent and experience the fantasies, conflicts, and object relationships that are the unconscious underpinnings of parental behaviours.

A great deal is known now on parenting; this knowledge comes from two main sources:

1. Psychoanalytic studies that cover issues such as the psychology of pregnancy and birth-giving (Bibring, Dwyer, Huntington, & Valenstein, 1961); the maternal contributions to the unfolding and to the pathologies of individuation–separation phases (Mahler, Pine, & Bergman, 1975); the parental contributions to early childhood pathology, which established the concept of "relational disorders" (Sameroff & Emde, 1985); the reactions of parents to the child's emancipation (especially in adolescence); and many other related issues.

Our own work has concentrated on conflictual parent–infant relationships as they produce behaviour and functional disorders in infants (Cramer & Palacio-Espasa, 1993). In all cases, parental projective identifications distort the representations of the infant, who appears in a light that produces anxiety in the parents, leading to defences and, secondarily, to pathological enactments (or interactions) that contribute to the infant's symptomatology. It is easy then to confront the parents with the distorting influences of their own conflicts on their interactions with their child that constitute— precisely—their parenting practices.

From the point of view of therapeutic practice, it is very useful to know in detail the derailments of parenting, their causes in the parents' own infantile conflicts, and their consequences in the many forms that pathological parenting can take. It is also important from the technical viewpoint to identify the types of conflict and defences that constitute parenting pathologies and the resistances and defences they entail.

2. Psychological studies of interactions, borrowing from ethological methods. Some parenting behaviours seem to be innate (like the high-pitched voice), and intuitive parenting (Papousek & Papousek, 1990) seems to organize many behaviours of adults when they are confronted with their young offspring. These studies are not dealt with here.

In this chapter, I report on our psychodynamic understanding of parent–infant conflicts and parenting failures; I also describe these parental difficulties and, especially, technical ways of handling them in conjoint psychotherapies. Finally, I provide some research data on the modes of interactions between therapists and patients in mother/infant psychotherapies.

Therapeutic setting

When the designated patient is a child less than 36 months old, he is seen with the parent(s) from the onset. We leave to the parent who contacted us the choice of coming alone or with the spouse. In Geneva, it is the mother who comes, most often without her husband. The mother reports on her difficulties with the infant, while the infant is either on her lap or playing with age-appropriate toys on the floor. From the outset, the setting is therapeutic: no formal history, following pre-set headings, is taken; the therapist remains rather unobtrusive; she listens to the mother's reports, considering them both as a source of (objective) information and as free associations. At the same time, she observes the infant and—especially—the interactions between infant and herself, and mother and infant. The therapist progressively tries to connect modes of overt interactions to the mother's discourse. This bifocal attention is a crucial technical device: it can often lead to an understanding of factors that have contributed to creating the infant's main symptoms, and this will be used in confrontations and interpretations.

Time plays a crucial role in mother/infant psychotherapies. Sessions need to be long enough (between 45 and 60 minutes) to allow for three developments:

- the creation of a working alliance;
- the development of a primarily positive transference onto the therapist;
- the accumulation of enough disclosures by the mother, and enough meaningful mother–infant interactions, to allow the formulation of a focus of interpretation.

Sessions are once weekly. The length of the therapy varies with the types of pathology. While borderline or severe depression pathologies in the mother require lengthy treatments, we found in a research on 120 cases (Robert-Tissot et al., 1996) that—to our surprise—a wide variety of cases including functional disorders (mainly sleeping difficulties), separation problems, and some behaviour disorders (aggression, hyperactivity) responded well to brief forms of intervention (from 5 to 10 sessions). Obviously, this short format depends also on the goals set by patient and therapist. In most cases, what mothers hope for is a relief of their anxiety about the child's symptom and a renewal of what could be called a rewarding relationship to the infant. In what follows, we will bring insights gained from these brief treatments in cases when there are no major (borderline or severe depression) pathologies in the mothers, and where the infant's diagnosis is not in the line of pervasive developmental disorders. In our clinic, these cases of functional and behaviour disorders constitute by far the largest proportion of situations seen among the children below the age of 36 months.

Without going into detail of the theory accounting for the briefness of such treatments, let us say that the explicit aim shared by parents and therapist is to unravel a focal conflict in the relationship to the child, without involving a systematic research of insight into the *whole* personality of the parents. One could consider these as focal therapies, the focus being determined by a specific failure in parenting, based on conflicts, and resulting in mismatches.

We discuss with the mother what the aim of the therapy is going to be: in most cases, parents do certainly not want to consider this a personal therapy, but they are willing to get involved inasmuch as the therapy will achieve two goals: clear the infant's main symptom and provide an understanding of the anxiety-provoking situation surrounding the parent–infant relationship. Thus, we explain that the aim is to understand what contributes to the symptoms, and that this requires some deep thinking on the part of the parent(s).

The child's symptom
and the mother's complaint

The reason for the consultation is always the infant's symptom: sleeping disturbances are the most frequent; behaviour disturbances are the second most frequent—the infant is aggressive, cannot stand separations, or is hyperactive. Feeding disturbances, breath-holding spells, or simply difficult, conflictual relationships can be the main complaint.

The wording of the maternal complaint needs to be studied in detail because the emphasis on certain details or descriptions, and the associations produced by the mother, will soon lead the therapist towards the beginning of a focal constellation that will become the main object of inquiry, leading to insight.

Some verbatim accounts of maternal complaints are presented below in which we describe maternal predictions, resentment against the infant, and painful affects of guilt and shame. The careful attention to words used is the same as in standard psychoanalysis: the therapist seeks to elicit the unconscious underpinnings of maternal representations of the infant, of various forms of anxieties or depressive affect, and of present–past links. It may be stated here that the use of video-recordings—allowing for typing the discourse and for repeated reviewing of sequences—is very helpful for the microanalytic study of therapeutic processes on the one hand, and of meaningful mother–infant interactions on the other.

The complaint contains one or several features that will orient the therapist's understanding: most often, mothers are anxious about the symptom. This anxiety takes several forms: dire predictions about the infant's future; resentment against the infant; painful affects; failure to understand the infant's motivations. Examples of these are given in full below.

Predictions

Mothers will express the fear that the symptom is the beginning of more severe psychic problems. This will contribute to predictions: if the infant is oppositional, this will lead to adolescent rebellion; if aggressive, this will become violence. Feeding difficulties are taken to be early signs of anorexia or bulimia, narcissistic omnipotence as predictive of tyrannical unruliness, and so on.

The mother should be immediately confronted with these bleak visions of the future, and the predictions should be unravelled and verbalized according to their most dire consequences. They hold precious information on maternal representations of adult psychic functioning which, unconsciously, belong either to the mother's own repressed wishes or to representations of people close to her (her mother, father, siblings, husband, etc.).

Example

"Sarah" is 13 months old. Her mother, "Mary", brought her because "She is developing aggressiveness . . . she has tantrums, she scratches me, bites or hits". Mary says that she does not understand where this behaviour comes from, and she is very anxious about it. Six minutes have hardly passed in the first interview when Mary develops a prediction about her relationship to Sarah and about the infant's potential character development: "Between us, it is like a power struggle; it is as if she was testing me. I would prefer that things evolve well between us. I would hate to see this lead to a dead end between us." Mary has already cast her child in a definite role, lending her intentions and representing her as a potential enemy. Moreover, she fears that this will lead to a breakdown of their future relationship. The extent of the prediction and its preciseness and rigidity are amazing when one considers that the infant is only 13 months old.

Mary goes on, adding: "If I started to give her spankings at the drop of a hat, she will stop trusting me; she will tell herself: 'My mother is a torturer' . . . and then it will be difficult to provide her with trust again."

The prediction is of a necessary development of sadomasochistic exchanges, with dire consequences for the relationship.

This type of prediction needs to be focused on and considered as a maternal projection, now attached to the infant. The preciseness of the theme, its repeated nature, all reveal that a sadomasochistic fantasy is at work in the mother. Indeed, we soon found that she had had repeated fights with her own mother, with reciprocal physical violence.

The therapist then established the link between the present conflictual relationship with the infant and the past sadomasochistic relationship with the grandmother.

Resentment against the child

Hatred against the infant has been underrated even in the professional literature, with the notable exception of Winnicott (1975). Most infant symptoms provoke irritation, leading sometimes to frank exhaustion and despair. Maternal sense of competence can be seriously eroded. The most frequent situation lies in the "syndrome of the tyrannical baby". The infant is experienced as demanding total submission to his whims and as wanting to impose his will while the mother must abandon all her rights. A very frequent complaint from today's mothers consist in an accusation of the infant as interfering with the mother's personal development, especially in the field of her professional achievements.

Example

"Delia" is 14 months old and presents a severe sleeping disorder. Her mother, "Maria", explains: "It started when I went back to work. She was 5 months old. She cried each time she saw me leaving for work. It broke my heart." Maria has just formulated her theory about the cause of Delia's symptoms: she feels abandoned when her mother goes to work. Now, it appeared that it was Maria's own representation of working and of her child's resentment that co-created the problem. Maria explained: "I hate to stay home merely to do house chores. Being a housewife makes me feel useless. I feel that I lost myself." Here, Maria defines a deep anxiety about a loss of identity when doing only house chores. She went on to complain about the baby who imposes intense demands on the mother, reducing her to the role of housewife. Delia is thus represented as a slave-driver, imposing humiliating tasks on Maria, while an identity based on studying and professional work is highly idealized by Maria.

This is the plight of modern mothers who have to lead a double career: mothering and professional work is a frequent source of conflict. The infant is resented because it imposes limits on maternal freedom and professional achievements.

In this case, it became clear that Maria tried to compensate her daytime abandoning of Delia by catering to her needs only at night, resulting in a sleep disorder. The night vigilance was also a defence against intense hatred towards the infant represented as a domineering and demanding slave-driver.

This hatred can lead to massive compensatory distortion, based on reactive formations against any aggression or authority. The "sacrificed" mother—while idealized in the nineteenth century—has recently been denounced in many feminist writings. The aphorism "Birth-givers need not become mothers" is a radical refusal of what had until recently been conceived of as characteristic maternal love (Ruddick, 1994).

All forms of maternal aggression against the infant need to be expressed and confronted with the greatest empathy and care. This is a very taboo subject as the collective representation of mothers is still intimately linked to unconditional love.

By far the largest number of sleeping disturbances in infants are linked to maternal fears of the baby's nocturnal death, and these are most often linked to unconscious hatred of the child.

Example

Delia's sleeping disturbance disappeared after Maria described her rivalry with her younger brother, whom she always felt jealous of. He went on eventually to university and obtained a prestigious diploma. Maria's complaint about not being able to pursue her career because of Delia's demands and pressures were linked to Maria's jealousy of her brother, who gratified his parents through his achievements. As we often find, there was a displacement upon the infant of a hatred and rivalry with the mother's younger siblings.

Painful affects

Anxiety and affects of the depressive category—shame and guilt—permeate the mothers' discourses while they talk about their children's problems and about their own difficulties in accomplishing their maternal functions.

The most frequent cause of anxiety is unconscious anger against the infant. This provokes obsessional preoccupation about the infant's health (fear of diseases, or death), of possible accidents, and of failures in psychological development (fear of autism, of mental retardation, of developing homosexuality, etc.). While fear of infant harm may have an adaptive function (in fostering vigilance and close attachment), it becomes pathological when it is compounded by neurotic conflicts. The infant may unconsciously represent a hated rival sibling, or a disqualified, repressed representation of the "bad" self of the mother.

Many other causes of anxiety can predominate, according to the mother's own conflicts. The mother may be anxious because she experienced the infant as very vulnerable, as demanding great care, or as needing ministrations that she feels unable to provide.

She may be anxious because she feels that she does not deserve to be a mother, due to unconscious rivalry with her own mother.

Becoming a mother may provoke a major identity crisis. She may experience mothering functions as destroying her former definition of herself. For example, she may have to abandon an identity based on professional achievements because she experiences it as incompatible with mothering.

This was well illustrated above by the example of Maria. She was one of many mothers who do not consider mothering an unmixed blessing. On the contrary, the tasks of mothering are experienced as a humiliating chore, and professional achievements are experienced as much more ideal and rewarding.

Many other forms, or contents, of anxiety may be categorized. In all cases, the source of anxiety has to be understood as evolving from the new imposition on personal resources provoked by mothering (Caplan, Mason, & Kaplan, 1965).

Guilt and shame

Although guilt has many unconscious sources, it tends to focus on the mother–infant relationship during the post-partum period. All the ambivalence, unconscious rivalries, and anger linked to important persons in the mother's past reawaken post-partum and link up with the representation of mothering and of the infant. Mothering is no longer the sole and main definition of womanhood as it was in the past, when it was said: "*Tota mulier in utero*" [All of womanhood is defined by the uterus]. This allows for more manifest—and conscious—expression of ambivalence towards the traditional mothering role. Mothers are no longer ready to sacrifice their personal longings for their infant, or, at least, not with the same excess and pleasure as in the past. But this does not go without corresponding guilt. Although the mother feels free to leave her infant in another's hands while she goes to work, she may nevertheless feel very guilty, thinking that the infant must experience this as an abandon. This guilt surfaces especially when the infant presents a problem or a symptom. Thus, mothers experience the consultation as an opportunity for confession, and as potentially redeeming them from guilt.

In Maria's case, guilt and shame were major contributors to what amounted to a mild form of post-partum depression (Maria scored 21 on the Beck Depression Inventory Scale). For her, going to work meant gratifying her own ambition while abandoning the baby. However, simultaneously, she felt ashamed when staying home "merely" to accomplish mothering tasks, because her family's ethics unilaterally emphasized the virtues of professional achievements. This led to an insoluble conflict, depleting her psychological resources. It was the interpretation of this conflict and of corresponding defences (among which her nocturnal hypervigilance was prominent) that led to two therapeutic gains: Delia abandoned her sleep disorder and Maria modified her representations of the infant as a slave-driver.

Resentment against the infant—which is more difficult to acknowledge than ambivalence about other objects—looms large in the determinism of guilt, as was described before.

Shame is mainly linked to feelings of incompetence in the mothering role. Mothers who consult about their babies project onto the specialist an ideal of total competence and knowledge about child rearing. This idealization gives tremendous power and authority to the therapist's pronouncements.

Many infant symptoms are experienced by mothers as a result of their incompetence. Shame is thus omnipresent during the first consultations. In our research on the outcome of brief mother/infant psychotherapies, we found that the most important improvement in the subjective state of mothers was a steady increase in their self-esteem after therapy. It thus appears that one of the main therapeutic ingredients in the process of these therapies is a shoring up of maternal competence. Maternal competence is far from an automatic given (like the now defunct "maternal instinct"). It can be terribly shaken, especially in primiparae. When the infant presents difficulties, this provokes doubt that is simultaneously determined by the mother's unconscious insecurity about becoming a fertile woman.

The therapist's work

In this section, I attempt to indicate along general lines *what* the therapist aims to do, and I provide some examples of *how* she does it.

First, it is important to note that the parent/infant therapist has a particular profile: she needs to have full training in adult *and* in child therapy, because she will need to intervene foremost with parents but should also be able to "read" the infant's contributions. Moreover, the therapist will need to know early development in order to understand the meanings of infant's symptoms, signs of anxiety, and modes of relating. A good awareness of interactive modes, as they are described in the relevant literature (Brazelton & Cramer, 1990; Emde & Sorce, 1983; Stern, 1984), is also very useful, as manifest interactions can be interpreted as modes of communication and as contributors to infant and maternal symptoms.

The therapist has to be able to listen carefully, as in a classical psychoanalytic session, but simultaneously she needs to observe overt behaviour and then try to match these two realms of productions. "Watching while listening" may be the therapist's motto.

The search for interpretation

The task of finding a main conflict, anxiety, or pathological mode of relating is much easier in parent/infant therapy than in standard individual therapy or analysis. This is now a well-recognized fact by clinicians who work in this field, while it remains a source of mistrust for therapists who work only with individual patients. The reasons for this remarkably easy access to core conflictual constellations are multiple; because they highlight the originality of mother-infant psychotherapy, it is worthwhile listing them here.

First, there is the now-famous surface access of unconscious contents in the post-partum period. This was recognized long ago, but it has received new attention from clinicians working in this field (Blos, 1985; Bydlowski, 1991; Cramer, 1993; Fraiberg, 1980) because it reveals a very particular, ad hoc, psychic functioning, only found in the postpartum mother. The mother's own infantile neuroses comes back to the fore, with powerful reawakening of images, fantasies, and conflicts belonging to her early relationship to her mother (and—to a lesser degree—to her father). Regression is loosened, allowing for old memories to surface. Moreover, the infant now provokes powerful affects, drive discharges, and archaic modes of relating. In fact, the demands made on the mother by the baby can act like a traumatic breach in the mother's usual defensive and characterological equilibrium. Maternal narcissism is shaken by the compulsive need to respond to the infant's requirements: she *has* to react, and she can no longer expect to impose her own initiative or incentive. This can be experienced as an enormous drain of narcissistic self-sufficiency and as a breakdown of schizoid defences.

The identity crisis of mothering

Moreover, following from the above, there is a redistribution of identifications. The woman finds herself propelled into the mothering, active, caring role, which can correspond to her representation of her mother or of her *ideal* of what a mother ought to be. At the same time, the presence of the baby—with whom she co-cohabited for nine months—induces regressive identifications to infantile states (dependency, oral greed, omnipotent narcissism, etc.). Thus, mothers may experience, side by side, maternal and infantile identifications, with corresponding fantasies and needs. This "identity crisis" contributes much to a loosening of usual identity references, which can be very painfully experienced, sometimes with verbalizations such as "I am losing my bearings", "I don't know what I am supposed to do". This contributes also to difficulties in deciphering the baby's motivations. Mothers often complain, "I don't understand why he acts this way". This epistemological quandary is due to secondary defences (inhibition, repression, splitting) against the emergence—within herself—of intense infantile needs, which she has to dismiss by externalizing them onto the baby who, thus, is experienced as "crazy".

A positive force

Finally, there is a factor that greatly motivates mothers actively to search for answers, and to collaborate in the therapeutic endeavour: their compulsive need to create a positive, health-promoting relationship with their baby. This positive force has been consistently described by Brazelton and Cramer (1990). They want to protect the baby from all sorts of external threats, but especially from the dangers imposed by their own neuroses and limitations. To be a good (enough) mother remains a very powerful incentive for realizing one's ideal. Moreover, the presence of the baby in the flesh—during sessions—has a tremendous impact. The infant's behaviours, demands, and affect expressions all bear heavily on the mother, fostering in her a sometimes frantic search for answers. Fraiberg mentioned that the presence of the baby acted like magic, "as having God on one's side".

The focus

Focalization is a main feature in all forms of brief therapies. While it generally refers to an active search for a central constellation that the therapist tries to capture, one can say that a focus is always the result of joint forces, where the therapist's search for interpretation and the patient's spontaneous production of a core, typical, and personal constellation meet.

From the first verbalizations of the mother onwards, the therapist is orientating her attention toward indices that, when brought together, could provide material for the creation of a core, focal constellation.

Clearly, the leading indices involve the infant's symptom; the choice of symptom is considered as produced by the mother as much as by the infant. It is her anxiety around the symptom that is the leading leitmotiv heralding the main tune of the conflictual music. One has to listen carefully to the words used to describe the symptom, the adjectives that are stressed, the emotions that accompany the complaint. Soon, a configuration appears, as on a stage, which introduces a major conflict, played out by more than two protagonists. Ghosts start to crowd the consulting-room, and one soon learns that they appeared as soon as the baby was born, or even before. These ghosts have characteristics of the maternal grandparents, or uncles and aunts; they may be inhabited as well by features of the father, or of the mother herself. She then sees the baby through an interposed representation of what is now—after Fraiberg coined the term—called a "ghost". The infant is stubborn "like my brother", or mean "like my father", or vulnerable and weak "as I was as a child", and so on. A story then unfolds, with the evocation of conflicts, of severe frustrations, or frightening anguish, or deadly fights. The unfortunate mother is then confronted with a baby that was intensely desired, but who becomes the emblem of anxiety, rage, or guilt. The representation of the baby vanishes, as it is invaded by former object or self representations.

These interfering representations can become very realistic to mothers because they are propelled by powerful projective identifications and externalizing processes. Mothers may then feel really persecuted or attacked by the baby.

The therapist needs to study these projective mechanism carefully: at one end of the spectrum one sees fleeting projections, with a prevalence of love cathexis over aggressive–narcissistic ones. It is then easy to undo the projection and bring back this projective identification into the domain of the mother's infantile neurosis. At the other extreme of the projective continuum, one can see very rigid projections, assigning mostly aggressive intentions to the child. This is much more difficult to mobilize, because of powerful unconscious guilt.

The object-related versus narcissistic dimension of projections also needs to be assessed. One of the most difficult situation is when mothers identify the infant with split of representations of themselves. What mothers hate then is a mirror image of themselves, embodied in the infant.

The definition of the focus owes a great deal to the projective identification process. The child is seen as incarnating a dreaded representation, causing secondarily a relational conflict with corresponding anxiety, guilt, and defences.

A first definition of the focus could be that it is made of a complaint about the child, a corresponding projective identification with corresponding conflict; this is a reawakening of a former conflict in the mother's past with original, primary objects. Anxiety of a specific form is triggered, with corresponding defences.

It is this "ensemble" that will be interpreted. The case of Maria and Delia can be used to illustrate the interpretation of a typical focus.

Example

The focus was interpreted 47 minutes after the onset of the first session. Much ground had been covered, many interactions between the three protagonists had taken place, and the therapist felt that she had arrived at a sense of conviction about the basic problem. This conviction was based on clinical experience, the repetitive evidence of the mother's basic conflict, affect manifestations, and the mother's responses to the therapist's tentative offers of verbalized understanding. The therapist then said:

"You see, I think that the sleeping problem is tied up to this. Because, probably, when you go to work—and we both know that this is a very important goal for you—it was in order to become *somebody*, to receive your parent's recognition, and to pay back your debt to them. You did this for yourself, in a selfish way—as you said—because work corresponds to a very important ambition in you. At the same time, you felt that you did this at the expense of your daughter, and I think that during the night, each time she cried, you told yourself: *I have to compensate necessarily with a nocturnal show of concern*, and you went to her immediately, in order to console her: *I have to compensate for her, because of what I withdraw from her when I am at work, and when I gratify my own ambition.*"

What is covered in this interpretation is mainly the unconscious guilt towards the child, the defensive behaviour of nocturnal hypervigilance, and the compulsive need to go back to work due to parental pressures.

Of interest is the fact that such a complex interpretation can be given in a *first* therapy session. This is typical of the powerful psychic reshuffling taking place in mother/infant therapies, allowing for rapid insight.

The role of overt behaviour:
mother–infant enactments

In joint mother/infant therapy, another original dimension is added: that of interactive materialization, or enactment. While the mother complains about the infant's symptom, the latter may precisely enact a "symptomatic interactive sequence" with his mother. When this—luckily—appears, the therapist obtains an added level of conviction about the symptom's genesis and maintenance, and this interactive determinant of symptomatology can then be demonstrated to the mother. The core conflict is then materialized, which adds an "acted" dimension to the scenario that unfolds.

The example of Sarah and Mary, given at the beginning of this chapter, illustrates what is meant by "symptomatic interactive sequence".

Example

While Mary is complaining at length that Sarah, her daughter, hits and scratches her, little Sarah is quite subdued, sitting on her mother's knees and pulling at a ribbon attached to her mother's sweater. At one point, Sarah brings her hand to her mother's lower lip and starts fingering it; Mary stops talking immediately and becomes hyper-alert, looking at Sarah. After a few seconds, she whispers: *"You scratch . . . don't scratch . . . give me a hug."* Sarah stops and drops her shoe on the ground. Mary asks, "Do you want to go down?", and she proceeds to put Sarah on the floor, facing away from her, towards the therapist. Within ten seconds, Sarah rotates back towards her mother and reaches for Mary's shoe, but Mary withdraws her foot immediately.

The therapist commented on Mary's expectation that contact with Sarah would be painful. The therapist noted that Mary had positioned Sarah away from her body, as if she wanted to avoid any physical contact. Mary acknowledged that she always expects pain in their contacts, adding: "I wish she would show tenderness. She never does."

Here, the symptomatic interactive sequence enacted the mother's projection of aggression and her punishment of distancing. It was also repetitive, as was demonstrated in subsequent sessions. The compulsive nature of this scenario and the rigidity of Mary's accusations against her young daughter suggested that she was "externalizing" an inner conflict onto the interactive sphere.

The main focus is often unveiled in the first session already; the process of the therapy consists in clarifications and in confronting many times the mother's manifestations of the main conflict, in making links (between present and past, between the representation of the infant and of the mother's imaginary partners, between the symptom and interactive mismatches), and in insights into the infant's subjective plight. Mothers are very often surprised to learn what the infant is trying to communicate, what its needs and anxieties are, and, especially, how much it is attempting to please mother.

When the main focus is well understood, mothers often "discover" the infant with new eyes, because the distorting effects of projections are lifted.

The aims of the therapy

It is important to note that these brief therapies have a definable and restricted goal. Contrary to standard therapy, it is not the whole mental set or functioning of the mother that should be modified. Rather, it is a specific sector that is targeted; this sector is the conflictual aspect of parenting involved in the precise difficulty linking *this* mother to *this* infant. The aim is to decontaminate the mother–infant relationship from its conflictual, unconscious underpinnings. The therapist knows when this is achieved: after a few sessions, the mother's anxious questioning abates and the relationship to the infant is experienced in a new way, with a renewal both of libidinal cathexis of the infant and of maternal self-esteem concerning parental competence.

Transference

These therapies can remain brief when the main transference is positive towards the therapist. When ambivalent, dependent, or hostile transference appears, long-term treatment is required. Interestingly, these brief forms of therapy are successful in part because there is a split transference: while the mother develops a strong positive alliance with the therapist, she simultaneously orients negative representations onto the infant, who is perceived as bad or damaged. Fraiberg had conceived this as a form of transference onto the child. When these negative representations are interpreted and re-placed in the context of their original objects, therapy can come to an end.

The therapist's contributions

These brief forms of therapies are worth while studying in a systematic way. First, they do represent a rather new mode of therapy, often bringing surprisingly good results, and this phenomenon needs to be evaluated as it can cast light on the nature of rapid therapeutic changes. It also can shed light on symptom formation and on the constitution and symptomatology of early mother–infant relationships.

Moreover, the brief format is easier to study than conventional psychotherapy: there are fewer processual vicissitudes and themes, and there are fewer intervening variables due to intercurrent life events and to developmental unfolding. This is an ideal format to study changes that can be attributed to the therapy process alone.

Our group embarked on a long-term study of outcomes and processes of 120 mother–infant dyads in psychotherapy. A comparison group was evaluated, undergoing a non-psychodynamic therapy (Interactional Guidance), in order to evaluate differentially outcome and process. The main results have been published elsewhere (Robert-Tissot et al., 1996).

In this last section, I provide some data revealing how the therapist contributes to the therapy, since this objectivization may help towards a specific definition of technique in this particular form of psychotherapy.

Amount of speech

Most psychoanalytically trained therapists expect to be very parsimonious in speech production. It is the undisturbed flow of associations—by the patient—that should predominate, leading the therapist to speak when an intervention or interpretation is safely anchored in the material and can be pronounced with profit.

The quantitative evaluation of patient's and therapist's verbalizations reveals that in brief joint therapies, verbal interactions follow a very different course. While the therapist starts on a low key, waiting for the material to lead the way, she will—after this first period of expectation—intervene often, in order to obtain material leading to the formation of an interpretative focus. When we looked at a typical first session and plotted the number of utterances according to the development of the session, we obtained the profile shown in Figure 7.1.

The configuration shows that each curve seems to be the mirror image of the other. One could say that the more one person talks, the less does the other. This is a complementary mode, typical for a conversation where reciprocity is respected.

This configuration reveals a harmonious exchange (akin to some shapes of mother–infant interactions) and is by no means the characteristic mode of therapeutic exchange. In some cases, the therapist is overwhelmed by the mother's productions and is reduced to a very low output of speech. In other situations, the therapist might be compelled to intervene more than the mother, because of the latter's resistance or inhibitions.

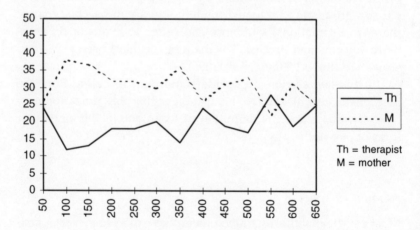

FIGURE 7.1.   Patient's and therapist's verbalizations

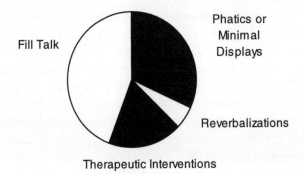

FIGURE 7.2.   Proportions of therapist's verbalizations

When one compares the total mean output of speech between the protagonists, one usually gets a distribution of 60 percent of speech output for mothers versus 40 percent for therapists. Indeed, these therapists are speaking much more than in conventional therapy.

Let us turn now to *what types* of utterances therapists produce. Three-quarters of verbalizations consist of minimal displays and fill talk (see Figure 7.2).* Minimal displays are utterances without meaningful content. Monosyllabic grunts are often used (e.g. "Uh, uh", "Yes", "Sure") either to show concern or empathy, or to indicate interest in a trend that the therapist finds relevant for further inquiry. These minimal displays are also called "back channels" by linguists, indicating the supportive nature of such verbal interactions. Fill talk is made of descriptive, factual, informative statements that do not carry an emotional message or a cognitive dimension—for example: "What is your daughter's name?" or "She hasn't slept for months."

*These findings are the result of research, "Therapeutic Process in Mother–Infant Brief Psychotherapies", funded by the Swiss National Science Fund, subsidy 32-40902.94. The following colleagues participated in the research: B. Cramer, C. Robert-Tissot, S. Rusconi-Serpa, F. Luethi, V. Wasem, A. Sancho-Rossignol, K. Bachmann, C. Champ, S. Genevay, L. Scippa, F. Palacio-Espasa, D. Knauer, C. Berney.

A small amount of intervention concerns re-verbalizations. This is a kind of reflective activity, used to show to the mother that what she says is pertinent, that it needs to be stressed, thereby indicating a need to go on more deeply in the same direction.

Finally, therapeutic interventions proper constitute less than a quarter of verbalizations. These are considered to be the specific technical activities of the therapist: comprehending, explaining, confronting and interpreting.

Analysis of the therapist's verbal productions underlines several points:

1. The therapeutic process results from an *interaction* between both parties, and not from the sole impetus produced by the therapist. There is mutual adaptation, common construction of a focus and of a working alliance, and a sharing of goals. These goals are attained by mutual regulation. The therapist supports the conversational exchange, she indicates interest for the development of certain trends, she shows empathy and understanding, she makes links, and—rarely—she interprets unconscious processes. The mother produces a flurry of affects and representations that crowd around the infant. She wants to find answers, but she also wants to please the therapist: these two forces work to create meaningful associations and a working alliance.

2. The therapist is more active than in conventional psychotherapy. She pursues hints, she unmasks avoidance, she creates links and prods for more confirmation. Most of all, she supports the unfolding of maternal revelations, looks for new directions, shows empathy, and demonstrates to the mother the infant's attempts at contact. The therapist manifests sympathy for the infant caught in psychic pain. She may play with the infant, or interact in a supportive way when his mother is upset. While she speaks more to the mother than to the child, she may also verbalize to the infant as if he were capable of understanding. For instance, she may say that the infant feels afraid when away from mother, or that he likes it when mother takes care of him, and so on.

3. The role of the child. A count of the number of verbalizations that the therapist addresses to the mother and to the child

shows clearly that these are largely addressed to the mother, who is the main partner of the therapist. However, we noticed an interesting phenomenon, typical for these therapies: the therapist, while talking to the mother, is constantly watching the child, as if monitoring its activities. Also, the therapist may simultaneously talk to the mother while playing with the child. We called this "double agenda". Whenever possible, the therapist will link the mother's preoccupation to the infant's activity or behaviour. In other words, the therapist attempts to keep the therapeutic focus at the level of the mother–infant relationship.

Some concluding remarks
about mother/infant psychotherapies

Early therapeutic interventions

The experience accumulated now by many clinicians concurs: mother/infant and parents/infant psychotherapies can obtain results that are both rapid *and* important. The rapidity is due to the flexibility of psychic structure in women during the post-partum period (which can extend up to 24 months in many cases). But briefness of therapy does not necessarily mean superficiality of effects.

These therapies, when they work, produce powerful transformations or even mutations of maternal representations concerning the infant and the maternal identifications. The flurry of projective identifications onto the infant can be very intense and distorting. Yet, these can be modified rapidly if the mother is allowed to bring forth the parts of her infantile memories that are reawakened by giving birth *and* by caring for a young infant.

The clinical experience of these therapeutic results, while not corresponding to the usual psychoanalytic ethos based on lengthy treatments and protracted interpretations of transference neuroses, indicates that interventions occurring in early development are a valuable tool for modifying conflictual relationship and, possibly, for preventing the installation of protracted conflicts. We thus consider mother/infant psychotherapy as a special therapeutic opportunity.

Learning about the beginnings of psychic structure

The detailed study of maternal projections and of corresponding interactions and educational principles sheds interesting light on the creation of "shared meanings" between mother and infant. It provides leads for the understanding and definition of furrows created in the infant's psyche, around which identity and fantasy themes may develop. The infant is embedded in a maze of meanings that parents assign to its daily experience—to what is pain or pleasure, what is forbidden or allowed, what is highly prized or despised. The practice of mother/infant therapy illuminates these processes, thus contributing to a conceptualization of parental influences on the building of psychic structure.

Evidence-based psychotherapy

According to Shapiro (1996) "evidence for the specific mechanisms adduced by adherents of seemingly effective therapy is typically surprisingly limited". I have provided in this chapter some research data on processes in mother/infant therapies which bring forth evidence for what actually takes place in these therapies. As discussed in more detail elsewhere (Cramer, 1998), therapeutic processes in these therapies show original features: in brief therapies, there is a need in the first sessions to formulate a focus. We could document that therapists and mothers work together towards the creation of such a common model or mini-theory. While therapists are mostly receptive at the beginning of a session, their output of speech increases towards the end of the session, and therapist and mother then share about the same level of speech output. Clearly, therapists are more active than in conventional psychotherapy (and, clearly, than in analysis). The main technical problem for the therapist is to determine a focus while not practising suggestion or manipulation.

When we looked at the types of verbalizations, we were surprised to find that therapists spend most of their speaking time producing apparently meaningless verbalizations, such as fill talk and minimal displays. One of the main lessons from this type of process research is that therapists are unaware of these low-level productions, which do not correspond to the idealized representation of the "inspired pronouncements" that, during their training, they had expected to produce.

Generally, we found that therapists are quite demanding of themselves (as was revealed in self-rating questionnaires). They over-idealize interpretations, whereas they underrate the importance of so-called non-specific ingredients of technique. Yet we know that many of these ingredients are destined to create a climate of alliance and to promote meaningful communication.

Finally, we found that the presence of the infant "in the flesh" plays an original role in the therapeutic process: the infant serves as a material, live prop for the mother's projections. When the therapist brings the mother's attention to the infant's manifestations (in what we called "double agenda"), she often discovers a new image of her child: for example, from a slave-driver, the infant becomes a benign human being capable of suffering and, even, of understanding. The distorting effects of projections are thus corrected, bringing about a more gratifying, less anxiety-provoking relationship to the child.

In conclusion, then, mother/infant psychotherapies represent one of many applications of psychoanalysis in the emerging field of infant psychiatry. They are both a valuable therapeutic opportunity and a setting for the study of infant development, mother–infant interactions, and psychotherapy processes.

CHAPTER EIGHT

Working with parents of sexually abused children

Gillian Miles

C hild sexual abuse is damaging and traumatic both for children and for their families. It often occurs alongside other forms of abuse—neglect, emotional abuse, physical abuse—but sexual abuse has its own particular emotional impact for the entire family.

When it occurs within the family, sexual abuse is secret and insidious, and the first impact of disclosure that the abuse has happened is a profound shock, which in itself is traumatic. Families are confronted with actions that cut across all taboos, as sexual abuse offends against the proper place of sexuality, which belongs in relationships between adults. There is total disbelief at what is emerging, because where the father or stepfather is the abuser,* there are profound implications for the adult partnership and for

---

The research referred to in this chapter was funded by the Department of Health and the Mental Health Foundation.
*Whilst recognizing the existence of female abusers and the abuse of young boys, throughout this chapter I restrict myself to considering the abuse of girls by male offenders.

his continuing role within the family. His partner feels irrevocably hurt. The children are considered unsafe with him, and either he or the child may have to leave the family. Where he denies the charge of abuse, his partner has to decide, in the absence of clear evidence, whether or not to believe the child, with the very possible implication that she will lose her partner. Almost more distressing, when there are allegations of sexual abuse between siblings, parents may have to decide which child to believe. The child alleging abuse may not be believed and may be forced to leave the family; alternatively, it could be that the abusing child is disowned and excluded from the family.

The emotional impact of such external events on vulnerable families is profound. Since child sexual abuse is a criminal offence, disclosure is usually followed in England by intervention by social services and the child protection team and by painful court proceedings, which in themselves can have a powerful traumatic impact. Partnerships can be broken, families split apart, homes and financial support lost. The families can be left with feelings of bewilderment, guilt, and shame. The non-abusing parent can be left feeling guilty that she did not know and did not protect the child. Feeling anger towards the abuser, she may also feel angry with the child, with a sense of having been betrayed and an intense experience of hurt and loss. Communication both within and outside the family about what has happened may be extremely difficult. Whilst being relieved from the experience of constant abuse, the child may have feelings of sadness about the loss of important adult figures in her life and of responsibility for the immense disruption to the family that the disclosure of abuse has precipitated.

Where the abuse is perpetrated by a stranger, the impact on family dynamics may not be quite so traumatic. However, the impact of the abuse is not necessarily lessened, as the abuser may be a trusted family friend. Most sexual abuse involves adults already known to the child and family, even if they are not family members; stranger abuse is less frequent. Much will depend on the severity and nature of the abuse, the age of the child, and how long the abuse has been happening. Much will also depend on the previous history of the family; on the strength of attachment relationships; on whether there have been other problems such as domestic violence or drug or alcohol abuse, on the patterns of previous relationships within the family; and on the parents' own early life experiences. The strength of previous attachments or the existence of previous difficulties within the family inevitably affect the family's capacity to cope with the trauma. The trauma of sexual abuse is also inevitably superimposed on the ordinary developmental hurdles of childhood development, and it becomes even more problematic to cope with where difficulties already exist.

The impact of sexual abuse
on the internal world of the parent

The external trauma can be so powerful that it is easy to lose sight of the impact of the sexual abuse of a young girl on her mother's internal world; it may also be too difficult to think about. Where the abuser is the father, the normal oedipal situation is totally disrupted; in external reality the child has displaced her mother sexually, and oedipal wishes have been gratified. Mother feels betrayed by her partner, and she is left to struggle with feeling betrayed by the adult alongside her sense of sexual betrayal by her child. Unconscious feelings of rage towards her own mother from her own childhood can be reawakened, together with anger towards her partner and her daughter, whom she is also wanting to protect. At the same time, the child may be both triumphant but also angry with her mother that she did not protect her. Where the daughter is an adolescent, the unconscious feelings of sexual rivalry between mother and daughter are enacted in reality, at a point when the mother is all too aware of the encroaching developing sexuality of her daughter, and when she is already preoccupied by the impact on herself and her own sexuality of her daughter's approaching sexual maturity and attractiveness. In the process of relating to her daughter as an emerging sexual adult, she is suddenly confronted by a child who has taken her place, an act of gross betrayal.

Whatever the age of the child, unconscious sexual taboos have been broken. Both mother and child are left with severe problems in their relationship, involving both conscious and unconscious guilt. The mother has to cope, too, with the fact that the child has knowledge beyond her years, and probably beyond her capacity to handle. The power of these unconscious forces leads to a sense of the unspeakable, a strong drive towards secrecy, and difficulties in communication within the family. When a young child has been abused, the mother, as a parent, has to handle her own feelings in order to be able to think about the possible impact on the child of inappropriate sexuality, and about the confusion that may arise for the child between parental love and inappropriate sexuality. In the eventual outcome, much will depend on the quality of the mother's previous attachment to the child. Much will also depend on the mother's own history, and the extent to which she has been able to handle previous traumas in her own life, since such unresolved traumas may well be reenacted in response to such a powerful situation. Furthermore, much will also depend on whether or not she believes her child, since this is of the utmost importance to the child.

Assessment of risk

It is against the background of such traumatic events that children are referred for psychoanalytic psychotherapy following sexual abuse. Given the essential nature of the confidentiality of the therapeutic setting, before setting out on therapeutic treatment it is important to establish that the child is safe from further abuse. In most cases this would mean that the abuser had left the home; or, if the abuser was not a member of the family, that everyone was confident that the child was protected from further abuse; or that the child was no longer in the family and was now in a safe place. However, it is also important to be clear from the outset that, within the treatment context, anything said that indicates the possibility of further abuse of the child must be taken seriously and can no longer be treated as confidential.

In some situations, it is very difficult to assess the risk of further abuse, since the mother herself may be extremely needy and torn between the wish to keep her children in her care and her need to retain a partner. The abusing partner, even while acknowledging the danger of further abuse, may long to see his children, and the couple may then be driven to subterfuge to retain their own relationship whilst the abuser continues to meet with the children in secret. In such situations, therapy is not possible as the child is not safe from further abuse. In any situation where there are doubts about the child's safety, it becomes essential to maintain close working links with other professionals working with the family, to ensure that the child is safe (Furniss, 1991).

Psychotherapy and work with parents in situations following child sexual abuse

It has been the established practice to offer parents time for themselves alongside their child's psychotherapy, to underpin the therapy with the child, to offer parents support and sometimes therapy in their own right, and, not least, to think about parenting issues. We have recently taken part in a psychotherapy outcome study in which girls aged between 6 and 14 years who had been sexually abused were randomly offered either thirty sessions of individual psychotherapy or between twelve and eighteen group sessions. The project involved eighty girls and took place in Inner London (Trowell, Kolvin, & Berelowitz, 1995; Trowell & Kolvin, 1999).

Alongside the girls' therapy, we were aware of the importance of offering work for the parents/carers. They needed to understand the impact of the abuse for the child, as well as the disruption to their own lives; they also needed to be able to cope with their stressful reactions. They were often faced with difficult or sexualized behaviour both within and outside the family. Relationships had been severely disrupted, trust needed to be rebuilt, and mothers/parents needed a space in which to have their own trauma and the disruption to their own lives acknowledged. Foster-carers were often managing extremely difficult, regressed, and sexualized behaviour in the contexts of their own families, sometimes with little support.

Overall, our object was to promote parental warmth, sensitivity, and support and, where possible, to restore the parent's confidence in their ability to provide good parenting and to provide a reliable attachment figure who could help their child to cope with the trauma of the abuse. In this context, we realized the need to acknowledge the parent's own difficulties, recognizing the depth of feeling and complex reactions likely to be present for them around the abuse, and the possible links between their attitudes and responses to the abuse and their own past experience. The work was with the mothers, with mothers and their partners, and with foster-carers, residential workers, and, at times, the children's social workers.

Given its short-term nature, this work was not seen as therapy in its own right, and it always needed to be focused around the present problems facing the family. However, for some it proved the beginning of a longer-term therapeutic relationship, since the work had allowed the parents to recognize their own needs.

However, in setting up the project, we had not anticipated the complexity of the work with the parents/carers, nor the degree to which we would need to work alongside other workers in the field to enable the children to come for their therapy. In many cases, it proved to be of vital importance to work closely with the family's social worker, enlisting the worker's support for the treatment, including practical help to attend the sessions, whilst safeguarding the confidentiality of the work for the child. We were very aware, in retrospect, that we had not anticipated the extent of the disturbance that we found in a high proportion of the families who came to the project, and we are unclear whether this group was representative of the overall range of families where sexual abuse has occurred.

Example 1

"Jane", a 13-year-old adolescent girl who had been sexually abused over many years by a family friend, was being brought regularly to therapy by her parents. The parents had been deeply traumatized by the discovery of the sexual abuse, and they were finding her sexualized behaviour outside the home, and her challenging behaviour at home, very difficult to tolerate. It was the school and the social worker who drew attention to the fact that Jane was again involved with an older man. Jane was excluded from school because of her provocative behaviour, and in the course of therapy she made suicide attempts. It was essential that the therapist was kept informed of these external events, and that the parents' therapist and child's therapist worked together with the outside agencies in their attempts to help Jane. This was not always easy as Jane's parents often felt attacked and criticized by the authorities and were themselves finding it very hard to tolerate Jane's behaviour. The conflict between Jane and her parents was often reflected within the professional network and needed to be understood and contained in order to help the family.

Example 2

"Ann", aged 10, had been sexually abused by her father from an early age. When referred for therapy, she was already in the care of social services, living in a Residential Home in the area. The workers in the home were very caring and sensitive to Ann's position, but they were alarmed to find that she was in the habit of visiting her father several times a week on the way home from school, and that her attachment to her father was still very strong. Until that time, they had not been aware how painful she had found the separation from her father. They themselves found her ongoing attachment to her father hard to comprehend since they felt so repelled by the abuse, and they wished to protect her. They needed the space provided by the carer-worker on the project to recognize Ann's strong positive attachment to her father and her consequent anger towards them for preventing her from seeing him. At times, they found it difficult to remain in touch with the extent of the pain of the situation to her, underlying her seeming composure and conformity.

Therapy for children who have suffered extensive sexual abuse can stir up a great deal of unbearable pain. Sometimes the children on the project became very depressed; at others, they acted out with very difficult behaviour, and at times they did not want to come to therapy to be faced with such feelings. At such points, the parents and the workers in the community needed to understand the possible meaning of their child's resistance if there was to be any chance of keeping the child in treatment; there were also, at times, concerns for the child's safety. All the agencies involved needed to work together, recognizing the importance of the treatment, despite the child's reluctance to come. The key person who held the bridge between the therapy and the outside world in the project was usually the carer-worker.

The impact of trauma

In all the activity, concern, and disruption that surrounds the family following disclosure of sexual abuse, the focus is necessarily on the child. Measures need to be taken to ensure the child's safety, but our experience within the project also highlighted the trauma experienced by the non-abusing parent. The knowledge that her child has been abused by her partner (or by a close member of the family) can be difficult to comprehend. As the child enters treatment, there is the opportunity for the mother to think about the impact of events on herself, often for the first time. With the secrecy that surrounds sexual abuse, and the deep sense of shame and guilt felt by the mother, normal channels of support and communication with friends and family have often been lost. Parents cannot talk to each other, and often communication between the adults and the child around the abuse does not take place. In this situation, the mother needs space to think about what has happened, and to acknowledge to herself the shock that these events have caused. Most often, in the midst of all the activity surrounding the disclosure of abuse, the feelings of the mother have become numbed and of necessity put on one side. Alternatively, she may be so overwhelmed by the impact of the abuse that she cannot hear the child. Acknowledgement of the trauma and of the overwhelming feelings involved is vital. Only when these are recognized and given time and space can the mother begin to think again, begin to pick up the pieces, and cope with the impact of what had happened.

Example 3

Mrs "Brown", the mother of four young children, discovered that her youngest daughter, aged 4 years, was being abused by her husband. She went through the investigations and court proceedings in a state of shock, and her husband left home. She was deeply shaken, unable to talk with her children, leaving them totally confused about what was happening. Mrs Brown was left for the first time to cope on her own with the children, the house, and the finances, and all the decision-making. When the therapists met with Mrs Brown and the children together for the first time, none of the family could speak about what had happened, either to the therapists or to each other; each one looked isolated, sad, and depressed. In the context of the unspoken abuse, the loss of the children's father, and her own distress, this mother could not be in touch with her children's confusion and anxiety. Any thought about the dynamics of what was happening was totally immobilized by silence about the abuse. Mrs Brown needed time on her own to gather and sort out her feelings before she could begin to help her children to handle theirs, to feel able to take on a more assertive parental role with her children, or to address her own depression and sense of worthlessness.

Example 4

Mr and Mrs "Jones" were informed by the school that their adolescent daughter had told a teacher that she had been sexually abused over many years by a close family friend. Although aware that their daughter had been having difficulties in relationships with her peers and was involved in inappropriate adolescent relationships, they were taken totally by surprise by this disclosure about someone whom they had trusted implicitly. Deeply shocked and angry, they could not talk to their daughter about the abuse, could barely believe that it had happened, and were faced with a disruption of relationships within the wider family. Both were in a state of shock, unable to think, and struggling with the impact on their lives of what had happened. The abuse had also placed pressure on their own relationship, brought up issues from the past, and led them to question their marriage and their ability as parents.

The trauma had to be acknowledged, and given space, before there was any possibility of moving on to think about the issues that the abuse had highlighted for these families.

The importance of family history and attachment issues

At the time of a child's assessment interview on the project, the parent/carer was seen and, alongside giving an account of the abuse and the family history, took part in the Adult Attachment Interview (Goldwyn & Main, 1996: this unstructured interview explores the subject's key relationships from the past, as well as issues of separation and loss; analysis of the interview is through analysis of the discourse). Following the assessment, the children were randomly allocated to either group or individual therapy. A clinical decision was taken about how often it was possible for the parent/carer to be seen: Some took part in weekly group sessions alongside their child's group, with a maximum of eighteen sessions; some were seen weekly alongside the child's individual therapy for thirty sessions; others were seen fortnightly or less often. About a third of the girls were in foster care, which had an impact on the allocation, as it did not seem helpful to have birth-mothers and foster-carers together in groups. Both children and parents/carers were seen for follow-up interviews one year and two years after the beginning of therapy.

There were, sadly, many families where sexual abuse was not a new phenomenon and where abuse had occurred across the generations. These mothers told of their own histories of sexual abuse, unresolved loss, neglect, and physical and emotional abuse. Out of this experience they had little sense of their own worth, and they had gone on to repeat past patterns and to marry abusive and often violent men. For these women, their own childhood experiences had been reawakened by the present abuse of their children, often overwhelming them in their capacity to think about the child. For some, abuse seemed almost an ongoing and predictable pattern of life. Where there was no sense that there had been a reliable attachment figure in a mother's life, it seemed a far more difficult task for her to provide a secure base for her child. Some parents seemed stuck in their own past unresolved traumas and abuse; others seemed able to use the sessions to think about their own distress and move on to be more available for their child's experience and emotional needs.

Example 5

"Helen", a 13-year-old girl, was referred to the project by her social worker following a passing incident of non-penetrative abuse by a family friend. She and her mother lived alone, following the violent breakup of a relationship. The mother was extremely agitated about the abuse and unable to maintain the relationship with her worker, or to support Helen's individual therapy. She was overwhelmed by thoughts of her own child-hood—which had been triggered by Helen's abuse—when she had been neglected, physically abused, and scapegoated by parents who were caught in a violent marriage and unavailable to her. Her sense of persecution was such that she could not use the space to reflect or to see the reality of Helen's depression and need.

There were many parents on the project who had themselves had traumatized lives and for whom the sexual abuse of their children had reawakened memories of their own past abuse and trauma. Many were lone parents, often isolated from their families, in which their attachments had always been strained. These mothers were struggling as sole parents to carry both parental roles. Some mothers within the project, however, had been able to move on to form new relationships that did not repeat the old abusive patterns. Despite difficult and abusive experiences in childhood, in many cases they were more fortunate than Helen's mother in that there had also been a good and significant attachment figure.

Example 6

"Clare", aged 9 years, was referred following severe abuse by her grandfather. Her behaviour was extremely disturbed, and she was difficult to contain in the children's group. Her mother was also very distressed and feeling very guilty, since she had also been sexually abused within the family as a child. Her uncle had abused her, and her mother had deserted her, but she described a close attachment to her grandparents, who had taken her and her siblings in later on, and she had cared for them lovingly in their old age. Her relationship with Clare's father had been violent, but she had recently moved on to a new relationship with a partner who did not repeat these patterns. She was able to use the parents' group to talk about her own abuse, her guilt, and her feelings about Clare's abuse, and to reflect and think about parenting issues. She was also able to stand back and allow her new partner to set clear boundaries for Clare.

Where a mother on the project had the backing and support of a new partner in parenting her child and in re-establishing the position of the parental couple in the child's mind, there were often considerable changes both in the child's behaviour and in the mother's self-esteem, her ability to handle her sense of guilt and to re-establish her own parenting role, and her own right to have a satisfying adult sexual relationship. However, it did seem significant that despite a very disrupted life, Clare's mother had had *some* good attachments in her own childhood and was able to go on to be emotionally available for her own child.

Parenting issues

Children who have been sexually abused can present severe challenges in their behaviour. Such behaviour can take many forms: inappropriately sexualized behaviour on the one hand, or, on the other, intense withdrawal, depression, and feelings of lack of self-worth. For many of the children on the project, the sexual abuse was but one part of their difficult life experience; they had often also experienced other abuse or deprivation. Some of the children had been removed from their families and, at the time of the therapy, were living in foster homes or residential care. For some, the foster-parents were providing long-term care for very disturbed and troubled children. Most of these experienced foster-parents were extremely committed to the children and were doing a good job. Even so, they greatly valued the support of the carer-worker alongside the child's therapy, and they appreciated the chance to think about the complexities of the child's life and the issues raised for them by the child's behaviour. They were aware both that the child had been abused and traumatized, and that she had also lost parents towards whom she still had strong feelings and who were important to her sense of her own identity. These foster-parents were able to acknowledge with a child the importance of the child's birth-families and her feelings about the past. They were also able to try to understand and contain the child's present behaviour in the light of past events and to provide the firm boundaries that had been so lacking in the past. For instance, a foster-mother needed to be able to think about angry and rejecting behaviour towards herself as possibly a projection of the child's anger with her own mother, whom she blamed for the abuse and for her inability to protect her. These foster-parents needed to be able to think and make links with the past when they and their families were put under strain by often bizarre and aggressive behaviour, or inappropriate sexualized behaviour, which tested them to the limit. The foster-parents also needed to know how to be available for the child, who needed to be aware that they were available to listen should the child want to talk about the past. At the same time, firm boundaries needed to be set around sexualized behaviour, which could place great pressure particularly on foster-fathers and on the other children in the family (Elton, 1988).

Where they also had contact with the child's parents at times of access visits, foster-parents needed to be able to respond appropriately to both the parents and the child. Indeed, many of these very needy parents also looked to the foster-parents for understanding and support; however, often they also needed to be given boundaries around the regularity and content of access visits. Given the sense of revulsion that sexual abuse arouses, it could be difficult for such foster-carers to understand and tolerate the fact that the abuser could be seen by the child as an important attachment figure, or that a neglectful mother could hold importance in a child's mind.

Example 7

Mr and Mrs "Green", who had been waiting for some time to foster children with a view to adoption, had only recently taken "Martin" and "Debbie", aged 11 and 7 years, when Debbie was referred to the project. The foster-parents were a thoughtful couple, who had been unable to have children of their own. They were a professional couple, with a comfortable house and lifestyle.

Martin and Debbie had been taken into care on grounds of severe neglect. Debbie had made allegations of severe sexual abuse by her father and by several others, and it seemed likely that their mother had been aware of the abuse at the time. The children, on arrival with Mr and Mrs Green, had many problems: their behaviour was sexualized, they were very chaotic, demanding of attention, and rivalrous with each other, and they found it difficult to adapt to new routines and a different lifestyle. For a time all went well, and both children seemed to settle into their new schools. At the point of referral to the project, the foster-parents were looking for help for the children and support for themselves in the transition.

When Debbie came into weekly therapy, the foster-parents were seen alongside. For a while, all went well, and Debbie seemed to respond to the new situation of therapy and be pleased to come. The foster-parents felt pleased with the extra support that they were given by the worker in the project, discussing how the children were settling in and some of the problems that had arisen. Although they found some aspects of the children's behaviour troubling, things seemed to be going all right. A great deal of thought and effort was going into settling the new routines and adjusting to new relationships within the family and the extended family.

As therapy progressed, Debbie became more in touch with her painful feelings from the past. Of the two children, she had felt closer to her mother, and she was intensely aware of the loss and an unbearable sense of rejection. In her mind, her mother loved and wanted her, and she longed to have contact with her, even though her mother made no response to her attempts to communicate. She also felt guilty that she was the one who, by disclosing abuse, had stopped her brother and herself from going home. She became very unsettled in the foster home and intensely rejecting of Mrs Green, with violent and distressing scenes. At the same time, she was quite sexually provocative with Mr Green, and by her behaviour she managed to create considerable tension between the couple.

The foster-parents were in a considerable dilemma. Mrs Green felt increasingly personally rejected by Debbie and found this very difficult to bear. Neither Mr Green nor Mrs Green found the sexualized behaviour easy to manage, and both, from their own past experience, believed in firm routines and standards. At the same time, they cared for the children and wanted to persevere. For a time the placement seemed in jeopardy, and they expressed their anger to the carer-worker, blaming the therapy for Debbie's deterioration. A great deal of work had to be done to support them in their parenting, thinking through-out about how to handle very difficult behaviour; however, centrally it was crucial to underline the importance of past experience for the children, and the importance of their birth-parents in their minds, so that the foster-parents could see the origins of Debbie's rage.

In this instance, the support that the foster-parents received, and their greater understanding that Debbie's behaviour was in part a displacement from the past, enabled the placement to continue, though it became clear that Debbie and her foster-carers would need further help in the future.

In such situations, the carer-worker needs to hold the sense of crisis, hopeful that it can be better understood and contained, enabling the child's treatment to continue. The work is dependent both on the sense of trust that has been built between the worker and the carer, and also on the capacity of the carer-worker and the child's therapist to hold and work with the anxiety created by the family within the treatment setting. Both workers carry powerful projections, which can mirror the dynamics within the family. It is important that as the therapy proceeds, the workers can evolve a pattern of communication that ensures both that the acute anxiety is contained, and also that the therapist is aware of any information helpful for the understanding of the child. However, at times of threat of breakdown, either for the family or the treatment, close communication between the workers is essential. Recognizing that work with the families of sexually abused children is extremely stressful, the project design provided regular supervision for all the workers. At points of crisis, a full team discussion would be held, chaired by a professional who was not directly involved with the family and therefore freer to think about possible projections and the process taking place. Again, when there was a crisis either at home or at school, the workers would decide whether it was important to attend case conferences with other professionals in the community. In doing so, we acknowledged the stressful role of the outside workers and the need to work together to ensure the safety and best interests of the child.

Family issues

In our experience within the project, sexual abuse was one of many issues for families who had struggled against numerous adversities. The sexual abuse was often superimposed on, and highlighted, other serious problems in the family's relationships. A powerful example of this was where the alleged abuse was by a sibling. Here the parental response was often very polarized; either the abuser or the child claiming to have been abused could be ejected from the family, whilst the remaining child was fiercely protected. The possibility of working to understand some of these intense projections, to think about the other painful issues within the family, and to effect change in the family dynamics depended in large degree on whether or not the carer-worker could remain working alongside the parents, in touch with their vulnerability and holding on to a sense of trust.

Example 8

"Mary", a cute little 6-year old, was referred to the project following alleged sexual abuse by her 12-year-old brother. The parents were outraged by his behaviour, and he had been placed in foster care. In their accounts, there was nothing good to be said about him—he had always been a problem. What had upset them most was that he had threatened Mary that he would kill her if she told. Mary was now frightened to go to bed on her own and, as a result, slept with her parents. She spoke very little but seemed to occupy a very powerful role in the family as the favoured child, apparently unperturbed by the fact that her brother had had to leave the home. Throughout the time that the couple were seen, there was little change in the way they thought about their son.

A fragile couple, they felt criticized both by their families and by the authorities; they refused to see the local social worker or to allow their son to come near the home. However, they gradually saw the project as a neutral place, where they were able to talk about their troubled marriage and their own experiences of neglect and abuse in childhood. The worker was able to begin to think with them about parenting issues for Mary: for instance, to get her to go back to her own bed, since it became clear that there were powerful uncontained oedipal feelings in the family, and it seemed that all thoughts about sexuality had been expelled with the son.

In other families, it was the abused child who had had to leave the home, when that child's account of the sibling abuse was not believed. In such situations, there was often a striking lack of communication within the family and an inability to talk or think about the abuse, or even about the absence of the missing child. Family meetings were not possible, but work needed to be done both with the child and separately with the parents in an effort both to understand the dynamics of what had happened and to contain the anxiety, anger, guilt, and despair.

In such dysfunctional families, where feelings are so powerfully polarized and where primitive defences are dominant, the therapists themselves, in their countertransference, can readily reflect the powerfully projected feelings, as well as being caught in a sense of hopelessness. The family rifts and conflicts can be mirrored both between the workers in the clinic, and within the wider network of professionals working with the family. Work with such families necessitates the workers' own struggle to manage and understand strong countertransference feelings, and sometimes such conflictual feelings between the workers, when understood, can throw light on the dynamics within the family (Bacon, 1988).

Cultural issues

Treatment of child sexual abuse in the family must take into account issues of culture, the traditional roles assigned to men and women, and the conventions and rules deeply held about the place of sexuality within that culture. When talking with parents, it has been important to be open to their understanding of the implications of what has happened. For instance, in some societies any suggestion that a father has sexually abused his child may lay him open to expulsion and danger to his life. The child may be viewed as irrevocably soiled and damaged, with a hopeless future. It may be the rule that such subjects as sexuality should not be spoken about with anyone outside the community or the family. The situation can become even more complicated when the family is living within a society that represents a different, more liberal attitude to sexuality and in which families find themselves on the edge of two cultures, two sets of rules. There are then nuances of meaning for the expression, say, of adolescent sexuality, and for the understanding of what is happening to relationships within the family.

The worker's therapeutic role

The parent's worker, in a clinical setting where sexual abuse is a factor, has the difficult task of holding together many different aspects of the work. The worker needs to hold in mind the boundaries of the treatment and the analytic work with the child; the continuing safety of the child from further abuse; the parent–child relationship and parenting issues; and communication with other workers who carry anxieties about the family.

Many studies have emphasized the crucial importance of maternal support and belief in the child following the disclosure of sexual abuse (Everson, Hunter, Runyon, Edelsohn, & Coulter, 1989; Green, Coupe, Fernandez, & Stevens, 1995; Newberger, Gremy, Waternaux, & Newberger, 1993). Sgroi and Dana (1981), writing about individual and group treatment for this group of mothers, spoke of their neediness, low self-esteem, lack of trust, and isolation. With their own past history of neglect or abuse, they have little satisfaction in their marriage, often a sense of disconnection from their bodies, and difficulties with sexuality. Consciously or unconsciously, this state of mind leaves open the way for children to be put in an inappropriate adult sexual role. Women who have themselves been sexually abused as children have often coped by either repressing the memories, dissociating them, or using other ways of keeping the memories at bay. If these mothers are to be available for their children in a similar situation in order to break the generational pattern of abuse, the worker needs to be available to allow them to think about their own experience of abuse.

Example 9

"Claudia" was 6 years old when she was referred to the project following sexual abuse by her father, who left the home with considerable acrimony. At the beginning, her mother was in an extremely confused, disorganized state of mind, shocked by the disclosure of abuse, and finding it difficult to cope with her daughter's distress. She needed support and containment, and she would fill the sessions with her anxiety and despair.

It began to be increasingly clear that there was a lack of boundaries between this mother and her daughter, and an inappropriate lack of separateness. As the work focused on day-to-day management issues, the relationship between the mother and Claudia, and the mother's own feelings about the marriage and the abuse, the mother gradually became more in touch with her depression and her own inner state of emptiness and despair. In doing so, she began to be aware of previously dissociated memories of her own sexual abuse as a child. The sessions became taken up with a painful remembering and putting into words of the detail of her own abuse, putting the memories into order, and linking the feelings to the memories. It felt like thinking the unthinkable, and the sessions felt unbearable, as she seemingly relived the experience in the safety of the therapeutic relationship. She got in touch with her rage with both her parents—with her father for his abuse, with her mother for her absence and remoteness. She became more painfully aware of the damage that had been done to her sense of herself and her own damaged sexuality. However, alongside, she became more in touch with the present-day realities of the repetitions in her life: her choice of partner, her frigidity within the marriage, and the sexual abuse of her child. Although at times her depression threatened to overwhelm her, at the same time she became more able to think about her child as a separate person, and to separate out her own abuse.

The impact of the work on the worker

Working with sexual abuse in this way evokes powerful feelings in the worker and can disrupt the capacity to think. Whilst it is important to be in touch with the projected pain of abuse, it is also important to be able to act as a container for the unbearable feelings (Kennedy, 1996). The invasiveness of the abuse itself, the profound impact on children's lives, the damage that is done, and the intensity of the feelings involved are often extremely difficult to tolerate and can threaten to reverberate within the personal experience and day-to-day life of the worker, and in the worker's life as partner and as parent. Working in abusive situations can also stir memories of abusive incidents in the worker's own past life, making it difficult to do the work. We were very aware throughout the project of workers' need for support and supervision, both to think about the families, but also to keep in mind the personal impact of the work and the workers' emotional well-being.

The role of men and of partners

Working with sexual abuse is to work constantly with experiences of harmful, bad sexuality. Very many of the women on the project, following abusive experiences in childhood, had gone on to choose abusive partners, thus reinforcing past experience of abuse and readily confirming an image of men as abusive. Subjected to constant projections about men as potential abusers, it could be all too easy for workers to collude.

However, there were some situations where mothers had moved on and found different non-abusive partners, who were actively involved in supporting them in the difficult role of parenting. Often such a new partner was able to help a mother, herself disabled by her own past abuse and guilt about her child's abuse, by setting firm boundaries, tolerating the child's distress and anger, and building good relationships with the child. In these situations it was important to acknowledge and confirm the partner's role, which held the possibility of breaking the generational abusive cycle and the assumption that further abuse was inevitable. The reassertion of appropriate adult relationships, with a benign father figure, although often difficult at first for the child to tolerate, held the potential for change, and for freeing the child to get on with her own life.

Groups for mothers

Within the project, we used two models: whilst most of the carers were seen individually or as couples, there were also parents' groups alongside the children's groups. These groups were run on the model of support groups, enabling parents to share their experiences of the impact of the abuse, to acknowledge their anger and distress, and to think about their relationships with their partners and their children. Hildebrand and Forbes (1987), in writing about such groups, talk of the powerlessness and low self-esteem of the mothers of sexually abused children and the value of addressing these issues within a group setting. Our parents' groups had two leaders, as we were aware of the intensity of the feelings that might be aroused. We were aware, too, that it was important to keep the groups homogeneous and that foster-parents and birth-parents would find it difficult to work together within one group. However, we also found that although the parents' experience could be shared within a group setting, and mothers could feel less isolated within a group, the more needy mothers found it difficult to use the group setting without making bids for individual attention, which could disrupt the group process. For example, within the group some mothers disclosed their own childhood abuse for the first time. Feelings within the group could become intense, with parents holding strong feelings about what had happened to other people's children. At the same time, group sessions were also a valued time for sharing experience, feeling less stigmatized by the abuse, and gaining confidence in parenting.

Conclusion

In discussing the work with the parents and carers of children who have been sexually abused and who have been in psychotherapy, I have described our experience on a research project where the children and their parents were offered short-term interventions, with at most thirty sessions of individual treatment. We were aware that for a high proportion of the families, the sexual abuse was superimposed on histories of neglect and physical and emotional abuse. Many of these families would not normally have come to the clinic, and their attendance was only made possible by the support of social workers in the community. Other children were living in foster or residential care, and the work with the carers alongside the children's therapy was with the foster-parents, and sometimes the children's social workers.

When the children and their carers were seen for follow-up one and two years after the end of therapy, it was clear that even such short-term interventions had been experienced as helpful; a number felt that it had been an invaluable support at a very stressful time in their lives. For some, the short-term intervention was enough; others went on to longer-term treatment. There was no doubt that the work with the parents alongside the children's therapy played an important role, both in sustaining the children's therapy, supporting and containing parental distress through the trauma of the abuse, and, where appropriate, giving space to think both about the relevance of their own childhood experiences and also about the parenting issues they faced with often very disturbed and troubled children. Our hope was that if the parents could be helped to resolve some of their own feelings, both around the abuse of their children and about what had happened to themselves in their own early lives, they would become more emotionally available to help their own children to work through the experience of sexual abuse, and so to free them to move on in their lives.

REFERENCES

ACP (1998). *The Training of Child Psychotherapists: Outline for Training Courses*. London: Association of Child Psychotherapists.

Alexandridis, A. (1990). Distorsion du pictogramme dans l'autisme infantile précoce. *Topique, 46*: 295–300.

Alexandridis, A. (1997). Paniques dans les psychoses infantiles. *Le fait de l'analyse, 3*: 51–60.

Alvarez, A. (1992). *Live Company: Psychoanalytic Psychotherapy with Autistic, Borderline, Deprived and Abused Children*. London: Routledge.

Anzieu, D. (1974). Le moi-peau. *Nouvelle Revue de Psychanalyse, 9*: 195–208.

Armbruster, M. A., Dobuler, S., Fischer, V., & Grigsby, R. K. (1996). Parent work. In: L. Lewis (Ed.), *Child and Adolescent Psychiatry: A Comprehensive Textbook*. Baltimore: Williams & Wilkins.

Aulagnier, P. (1975). *La violence de l'interpretation: du pictogramme à l'énonce*. Paris: Presses Universitaires de France.

Bachelard, G. (1972). *La formation de l'esprit scientifique*. Paris: Vrin.

Bacon, R. (1988). Countertransference in a case conference: resistance and rejection in work with abusing families and their children. In:

G. Pearson, J. Treseder, & M. Yelloly (Eds.), *Social Work and the Legacy of Freud*. London: Macmillan.

Barrows, P. (1995). Oedipal issues at 4 and 44. *Psychoanalytic Psychotherapy, 9* (1): 85–96.

Benedek, T. (1959). Parenthood as a developmental phase. *Journal of the American Psychoanalytic Association, 7*: 389–417.

Bettelheim, B. (1967). *The Empty Fortress: Infantile Autism and the Birth of the Self*. New York: Free Press.

Bibring, G., Dwyer, T. F., Huntington, D. S., & Valenstein, A. F. (1961). A study of psychological processes in pregnancy of the earliest mother–child relationship. *Psychoanalytic Study of the Child, 16*: 9–27.

Bion, W. R. (1961). *Experiences in Groups and Other Papers*. London: Tavistock Publications.

Bion, W. R. (1962a). A theory of thinking. *International Journal of Psycho-Analysis, 43*: 306–310. Also in: *Second Thoughts*. London: Heinemann, 1967 [reprinted London: Karnac Books, 1984].

Bion, W. R. (1962b). *Learning from Experience*. London: Heinemann [reprinted London: Karnac Books, 1984].

Block Lewis, H. (1987). Shame and the narcissistic personality. In: D. L. Nathanson (Ed.), *The Many Faces of Shame*. New York: Guilford Press.

Blos, P. J. (1985). Intergenerational separation-individuation. Treating the mother–infant pair. *Psychoanalytic Study of the Child, 40*: 41–56.

Brazelton, T. B., & Cramer, B. (1990). *The Earliest Relationship*. Reading, MA: Addison-Wesley [reprinted London: Karnac Books, 1992].

Brentano, F. (1874). *Psychology from an Empirical Standpoint*. London: Routledge, 1995.

Bydlowski, M. (1991). La transparence psychique de la grossesse. *Etudes Freudiennes, 32*: 135–142.

Caplan, G., Mason, E. A., & Kaplan, D. M. (1965). Four studies of crisis in parents of prematures. *Community Mental Health Journal, 1*: 149–161.

Carlberg, G. (1985). *Psykoterapi med fšršldrar till psykotiska barn* [Psychotherapy with parents of psychotic children]. Stockholm: Svenska fšreningen fšr psykisk hšlsovœrds, Monograph No. 21.

Chaffin, R., & Winston, M. (1991). Conceptions of parenthood. *Journal of Applied Social Psychology, 21*: 1726–1757.

Churchill, D. (1972). The relation of infantile autism and early childhood schizophrenia to developmental language disorders of childhood. *Journal of Autism and Childhood Schizophrenia, 2*: 182–197.

Copley, B. (1987). Explorations with families. *Journal of Child Psychotherapy, 13* (1): 93–108.

Cramer, B. (1993). Are postpartum depressions a mother–infant relationship disorder? *Infant Mental Health Journal, 14* (4): 283–297.

Cramer, B. (1995). Short-term dynamic psychotherapy for infants and their parents. In: K. Minde (Ed.), *Child and Adolescent Psychiatric Clinics of North America, 4* (3): 649–660.

Cramer, B. (1998). Mother–infant psychotherapies: a widening scope in technique. *Infant Mental Health Journal, 19* (2): 151–167.

Cramer, B., & Palacio-Espasa, F. (1993). *La Pratique des psychothérapies mères–bébés*. Paris: Presses Universitaires de France.

Daws, D. (1989). *Through the Night: Helping Parents and Sleepless Infants*. London: Free Association Books.

Dawson, G. (Ed.) (1989). *Autism: Nature, Diagnosis, and Treatment*. London: Guilford Press.

Elton, A. (1988). Working with substitute carers. In: A. Bentovim, A. Elton, J. Hildebrand, M. Tranter, & E. Vizard (Eds.), *Child Sexual Abuse within the Family: Assessment and Treatment* (pp. 238–251). London: Wright.

Emde, R. N., & Sorce, J. E. (1983). The rewards of infancy: emotional availability and maternal referencing. In: J. D. Call, E. Galenson, & R. Tyson (Eds.), *Frontiers of Infant Psychiatry, Vol. 2*. New York: Basic Books.

Everson, M., Hunter, W., Runyon, D., Edelsohn, G., & Coulter, P. (1989). Maternal support following disclosure of incest. *American Journal of Orthopsychiatry, 59* (2): 197–207.

Fenichel, O. (1946). *The Psychoanalytic Theory of Neurosis*. London: Routledge, 1990.

Fonagy, P., & Target, M. (1996). Predictors of outcome in child psychoanalysis: a retrospective study of 763 cases at the Anna Freud Centre. *Journal of the American Psychoanalytic Association, 44*: 27–73.

Fraiberg, S. (1980). *Clinical Studies in Infant Mental Health: The First Year of Life*. New York: Basic Books.

Fraiberg, S. (1987). *Selected Writings of Selma Fraiberg*, ed. L. Fraiberg. Columbus, OH: Ohio State University Press.

Freud, S. (1895d) (with Breuer, J.). *Studies on Hysteria. S.E., 2*.

Freud, S. (1940a [1938]). *An Outline of Psycho-Analysis. S.E., 23*.

Furman, E. (1957). Treatment of under fives by way of parents. *Psycho-analytic Study of the Child, 12*: 250–262.

Furman, E. (1966). "Parenthood as a Developmental Phase." Paper presented at the first scientific meeting of the Association for Child Psychoanalysis, Topeka, KS (Spring).

Furman, E. (1991). Treatment-via-the-parent: a case of bereavement. In: R. Szur & S. Miller (Eds.), *Extending Horizons: Psychoanalytic Psychotherapy with Children, Adolescents and Families*. London: Karnac Books.

Furniss, T. (1991). *The Multi Professional Handbook of Child Sexual Abuse*. London: Routledge.

Gibbs, I. (1998). "A Second Chance for Emma." Unpublished paper on non-intensive work for qualification as a child psychotherapist with the BAP.

Goldwyn, R., & Main, M. (1996). *Adult Attachment Scoring: A Classification System for Assessing Attachment Organisation through Discourse*. Cambridge: Cambridge University Press.

Green, A., Coupe, P., Fernandez, R., & Stevens, B. (1995). Incest revisited: delayed post-traumatic stress disorder in mothers following the sexual abuse of their children. *Child Abuse and Neglect, 19* (10): 1275–1282.

Greenson, R. R. (1967). *The Technique and Practice of Psychoanalysis*. New York: International Universities Press.

Harris, M. (1968). The child psychotherapist and the patient's family. *Journal of Child Psychotherapy, 2* (2): 50–63.

Harris, M. (1975). Some notes on maternal containment in *Good Enough Mothering. Journal of Child Psychotherapy, 4* (1): 35–51.

Hesselman, S. (1992). Motšverfšring vid barn- och ungdomspsykoterapi. Presentation av litteratur om ett fšrsummat begrepp [Countertransference in child- and adolescent psychotherapy—presentation of literature on a neglected concept]. Stockholm: Ericastiftelsen Rapport 2.

Hildebrand, J., & Forbes, C. (1987). Group work with mothers who have been sexually abused. *British Journal of Social Work, 17* (3): 285–303.

Hobson, R. P. (1989). Beyond cognition: a theory of autism. In: G. Dawson (Ed.), *Autism: Nature, Diagnosis, and Treatment* (pp. 22–48). London: Guilford Press.

Hobson, R. P. (1993). *Autism and the Development of Mind*. Hove: Laurence Erlbaum.

Hopkins, J. (1992). Infant–parent psychotherapy. *Journal of Child Psychotherapy, 18*: 5–19.

Horne, A. (1999). Sexual abuse and sexual abusing in childhood and adolescence. In: M. Lanyado & A. Horne (Eds.), *Handbook of Child & Adolescent Psychotherapy: Psychoanalytic Approaches.* London: Routledge.

Houzel, D. (1986). Un élément du cadre: l'alliance thérapeutique. *Journal de la Psychanalyse de l'enfant, 2*: 78–94.

Kanner, L. (1943). Autistic disturbances of affective contact. In: *Childhood Psychosis: Initial Studies and New Insights.* Washington, DC: Winston & Sons, 1973.

Kennedy, R. (1996). Bearing the unbearable: working with the abused mind. *Psychoanalytic Psychotherapy, 10* (2): 143–154.

Klauber, T. (1998). The significance of trauma in work with the parents of severely disturbed children, and its implications for work with parents in general. *Journal of Child Psychotherapy, 24* (1): 85–107.

Klein, M. (1946). Notes on some schizoid mechanisms. *International Journal of Psycho-Analysis, 27*: 99–110. Also in: *Envy and Gratitude and Other Works.* London: Hogarth Press, 1975 [reprinted London: Karnac Books, 1993.]

Klein, M. (1932). The technique of analysis in the latency period. In: *The Psychoanalysis of Children* (revised edition, 1975). London: Hogarth Press [reprinted London: Karnac Books, 1998].

Klein, M. (1935). A contribution to the psychogenesis of manic-depressive states. *International Journal of Psycho-Analysis, 16*: 145–174. Also in: *Love, Guilt and Reparation and Other Works 1921–1945.* London: Hogarth Press, 1975 [reprinted London: Karnac Books, 1992.]

Klein, M. (1988). *Love, Guilt and Reparation and Other Works 1921–1945* (with a new introduction by Hanna Segal). London: Virago Press [reprinted London: Karnac Books, 1992].

Kohrman, R., Fineberg, H., Gelman, R., & Weiss, S. (1971). Technique of child analysis: problems of countertransference. *International Journal of Psycho-Analysis, 52*: 487.

Kolvin, I., & Trowell, J. (1996). Child sexual abuse. In: I. Rosen (Ed.), *Sexual Deviation* (3rd edition). Oxford: Oxford University Press.

Lebovici, S. (1983). *Le nourrisson, la mère et le psychanalyste. Les interactions précoces.* Paris: Paidos, Le Centurion.

Leslie, A. M., & Frith, U. (1988). Autistic children's understanding of seeing, knowing and believing. *British Journal of Developmental Psychology, 4:* 315–324.

Lieberman, A. F., Weston, D. R., & Pawl, J. H. (1991). Preventive intervention and outcome with anxiously attached dyads. *Child Development, 62* (1): 205–208.

Lovaas, O. (1977). *The Autistic Child: Language Development through Behavior Modification.* New York: Wiley.

Mahler, M. (1968). *On Human Symbiosis and the Vicissitudes of Individuation, Vol. 1: Infantile Psychosis.* New York: International Universities Press.

Mahler, M. S., Pine, F., & Bergman, A. (1975). *The Psychological Birth of the Human Infant.* New York: Basic Books [reprinted London: Karnac Books, 1988].

Maratos, O. (1997). Psychoanalysis and the management of pervasive developmental disorders. In: C. Trevarthen, K. Aitken, D. Papoudi, & J. Robarts (Eds.), *Children with Autism* (pp. 161–171). London: Jessica Kingsley.

Meltzer, D., Bremner, J., Hoxter, S., Weddell, D., & Wittenberg, I. (1975). *Explorations in Autism: A Psycho-Analytical Study.* Perthshire: Clunie Press.

Miller, L. (1992). The relation of infant observation to clinical practice in an under-fives counselling service. *Journal of Child Psychotherapy, 18* (1): 19–32.

Morrison, A. P. (1983). Shame, ideal self, and narcissism. *Contemporary Psychoanalysis, 19:* 295–318.

Newberger, C., Gremy, I., Waternaux, C., & Newberger, I. (1993). Mothers of sexually abused children: trauma and repair in longitudinal perspective. *American Journal of Orthopsychiatry, 63* (1): 92–102.

Offerman-Zuckerberg, J. (1992). The parenting process: a psychoanalytic perspective. *Journal of the American Academy of Psychoanalysis, 20:* 205–214.

Ornstein, A. (1976). Making contact with the inner world of the child. *Comprehensive Psychiatry, 17:* 3–36.

Papousek, M., & Papousek, H. (1990). Excessive infant crying and intuitive parental care: buffering support and its failures in parent–infant interaction. *Early Child Development and Care, 63:* 117–126.

Pines, D. (1993). *A Woman's Unconscious Use of Her Body: Psychoanalytic Approaches.* London: Virago.

Rimland, B. (1964). *Infantile Autism.* New York: Appleton-Century-Crofts.

Robert-Tissot, C., Cramer, B., Stern, D. N., Rusconi-Serpa, S., Bachmann, J.-P., Palacio-Espasa, F., Knauer, D., De Muralt, M., Berney, C., & Mendiguren, G. (1996). Outcome evaluation in brief mother–infant psychotherapies: report on 75 cases. *Infant Mental Health Journal, 17* (2): 97–114.

Ruddick, S. (1994). Thinking mothers/conceiving birth. In: D. Bassin, M. Honey, & M. M. Kaplan (Eds.), *Representations of Motherhood.* New Haven, CT: Yale University Press.

Rustin, M. (1999). The place of consultation with parents and therapy of parents in child psychotherapy practice. In: M. Lanyado & A. Horne (Eds.), *Handbook of Child & Adolescent Psychotherapy: Psychoanalytic Approaches.* London: Routledge.

Ruszczynski, S. (1993). Thinking about and working with couples. In: S. Ruszczynski (Ed.), *Psychotherapy with Couples.* London: Karnac Books.

Rutter, M. (1978). Diagnosis and definition of childhood autism. *Journal of Autism and Developmental Disorders, 8*: 139–161.

Rutter, M. (1983). Cognitive deficits in the pathogenesis of autism. *Journal of Child Psychology and Psychiatry, 24*: 513–531.

Salzberger-Wittenberg, I. (1970). *Psycho-Analytic Insight and Relationships—A Kleinian Approach.* London: Routledge & Kegan Paul.

Sameroff, A., & Emde, R. (1985). *Relationship Disturbances in Early Childhood: A Developmental Approach.* New York: Basic Books.

Sgroi, S. M., & Dana, N. T. (1984). Individual and group treatment of mothers of incest victims. In: S. M. Sgroi (Ed.), *Handbook of Clinical Intervention in Child Sexual Abuse.* Lexington, MA: Lexington Books.

Shapiro, D. (1996). Foreword. In: A. Ruth, & P. Fonagy (Eds.), *What Works For Whom? A Critical Review of Psychotherapy Research.* New York: Guilford Press.

Shuttleworth, A. (1982). "Finding a Way to the Parent." Unpublished paper given at the Inter-Clinic Conference (October) as part of a Tavistock Clinic contribution on "Concepts of Change".

Simcox-Reiner, B., & Kaufman, I. M. D. (1959). *Character Disorders in*

Parents of Delinquents. New York: Family Service Association of America.

Stern, D. N. (1984). *The Interpersonal World of the Infant.* New York: Basic Books [reprinted London: Karnac Books, 1999].

Stern, D. N. (1995). *The Motherhood Constellation: A Unified View of Parent–Infant Psychotherapy.* New York: Basic Books [reprinted London: Karnac Books, 1999].

Tischler, S. (1971). Clinical work with the parents of psychotic children. *Psychiatry, Neuralgia, Neurochirurgia, 74:* 225–249.

Tischler, S. (1979). Being with a psychotic child: a psychoanalytical approach to the problems of parents of psychotic children. *International Journal of Psycho-Analysis, 60* (1): 29–38.

Trevarthen, C. (1993). The function of emotions in early infant communication and development. In: J. Nadel & L. Camaioni (Eds.), *New Perspectives in Early Communicative Development.* London: Routledge.

Trevarthen, C., Aitken, K., Papoudi, D., & Robarts, J. (1996). *Children with Autism.* London: Jessica Kingsley.

Trowell, J., & Kolvin, I. (1999). Lessons from a psychotherapy outcome study with sexually abused girls. *Journal of Clinical Child Psychology and Psychiatry, 4* (1): 79–89.

Trowell, J., Kolvin, I., & Berelowitz, M. (1995). Design and methodological issues in a psychotherapy outcome study with sexually abused girls. In: M. Aveline & D. Shapiro (Eds.), *Research Foundations for Psychotherapy Practice.* Chichester: Wiley [in association with the Mental Health Foundation].

Tustin, F. (1972). *Autism and Childhood Psychosis.* London: Hogarth Press [reprinted London: Karnac Books, 1996].

Tustin, F. (1981). *Autistic States in Children.* London: Routledge.

van der Pas, A. (1996). Naar een psychologie van ouderschap. Besef van verantwoordelijk zijn [Towards a psychology of parenthood. Realization of being responsible.] In: *Handboek Methodische Ouderbegeleiding 2.* Rotterdam: Ad. Donker bv.

Waksman, J. (1986). The countertransference of the child analyst. *International Review of Psycho-Analysis, 13:* 405.

Winnicott, D. W. (1955). The depressive position in normal emotional development. *British Journal of Medical Psychology, 28:* 89–100. Also in: *Through Paediatrics to Psycho-Analysis.* London: Tavistock Publications, 1958 [reprinted London: Karnac Books, 1992].

Winnicott, D. W. (1960). The theory of the parent–infant relationship. *International Journal of Psycho-Analysis, 41*: 585–595. Also in: *The Maturational Processes and the Facilitating Environment.* London: Hogarth Press, 1965 [reprinted London: Karnac Books, 1990].

Winnicott, D. W. (1963). The development of the capacity for concern. *Bulletin of the Menninger Clinic, 27*: 167–176. Also in: *The Maturational Processes and the Facilitating Environment.* London: Hogarth Press, 1965 [reprinted London: Karnac Books, 1990].

Winnicott, D. W. (1965). *The Family and Individual Development.* London: Tavistock Publications.

Winnicott, D. W. (1971). *Therapeutic Consultations in Child Psychiatry.* London: Hogarth Press [reprinted London: Karnac Books, 1996].

Winnicott, D. W. (1975). Hate in the countertransference. In: *Through Paediatrics To Psychoanalysis.* London: Hogarth Press [reprinted London: Karnac Books, 1992.]

Zetzel, E. (1956). Current concepts of transference. *International Journal of Psycho-Analysis, 37*: 369–376.

INDEX